The LITTLE PRINCESSES

The story of the Queen's childhood,
by her nanny

MARION CRAWFORD

Introduced by Jennie Bond

An Orion paperback

First published in Great Britain in 1950
by Cassell & Co Ltd
This edition published in 2002
by Orion
This paperback edition published in 2003
by Orion Books Ltd,

Carmelite House, 50 Victoria Embankment
London EC4Y 0DZ

10

A CIP catalogue record for this book
is available from the British Library.

ISBN 978-0-7528-4974-4

Printed and bound in Great Britain by
Clays Ltd, Elcograf S.p.A.

www.orionbooks.co.uk

Contents

For fourteen years Jennie Bond followed the Royal Family as the BBC's Royal Correspondent. In that time, she covered many momentous events – among them, three marriage breakdowns, Camillagate, the Queen's annus horribilis and the death of the Princess of Wales, whom Jennie had met privately on a number of occasions.

List of Plates

The Master of Carnegie's sixth birthday party
Riding with their father in Windsor Great Park
Princess Elizabeth at London Zoo
A game of 'horses and carts' with Margaret Elphinstone
Arriving at the underground station
Glamis Castle
The Princesses about to work on their garden plots

The Royal Family in their Coronation robes
The Coronation procession at Westminster Abbey,
    12 May 1937
On the balcony of Buckingham Palace
A trip on the Thames
A pony show at London's Agricultural Hall
The Princesses at Royal Lodge setting out for a morning ride
Princess Margaret on a voyage downriver
Balmoral Castle
Something catches Princess Margaret's eye
In the garden of Royal Lodge, Windsor
Princess Elizabeth did not find knitting easy
Princess Margaret leaving a bazaar at Crathie Church
Princess Margaret at a Welsh Pit Ponies' Display
Princess Elizabeth sits for the sculptor, K. S. de Strobl
The Royal Family at Portsmouth
A studio portrait of Princess Margaret, aged eight
The Princesses with Crawfie aboard a destroyer
Princess Elizabeth life-saving at the Bath Club, London
Marion Crawford
A dress rehearsal of the Aldershot Tattoo
Community singing during a visit to the King's Camp
    at Abergeldie
The Princesses with their outsize jigsaw puzzle

Acknowledgements

Grateful acknowledgement is made to the following for the use of photographs in this book:

> Marcus Adams
> Associated Press Ltd
> Baron Studios
> Central Press Photos Ltd
> Fox Photos Ltd
> Graphic Photo Union
> Harris's Picture Agency
> Imperial War Museum
> Keystone Press Agency Ltd
> The London Electrotype Agency Ltd
> London News Agency Photos Ltd
> Mirrorpic
> New York Times Photos
> PA–Reuter Photos
> Studio Lisa
> The Times
> Topical Press Agency Ltd
> Dorothy Wilding

Foreword

DURING more than a decade as royal correspondent for the BBC I have waged many a battle with Buckingham Palace over access to information. I have berated and badgered a succession of press secretaries, demanding answers to my questions. Slowly and grudgingly the Palace doors have opened enough to allow a chink of light inside. The process has been given the odd unexpected boost by one or two members of the Royal Family who've volunteered to 'go public' with astonishing personal revelations. There remains, however, a deep scepticism within the Palace walls about the media and their function in reporting on royalty. Greater still is the horror with which any member of staff who 'spills the beans' is viewed.

Patrick Jephson, who gave his account of life as private secretary to the Princess of Wales, was seen as a traitor to her memory. Wendy Berry, a former housekeeper at Highgrove, was forced to flee to Canada when she published a book that was described to me by someone in the household as the most accurate record of the final years of the Wales's marriage. But the pioneer of the royal 'kiss and tell' was undoubtedly Marion Crawford, governess and confidante of Lilibet, the young girl who would one day become Queen, and of her sister Margaret.

The Little Princesses is a charming, hopelessly romantic

chronicle of 'Crawfie's' life during sixteen years at the heart of the Royal Family. It is also a valuable piece of social history, detailing every aspect of Elizabeth and Margaret's childhood through the crucial years of the Abdication and the war as well as Lilibet's courtship and marriage.

It is harmless in the extreme: among the most 'explosive' revelations is the fact that in the schoolroom the two Princesses behaved like entirely normal and healthy little girls. 'Neither was above taking a whack at her adversary, if roused, and Lilibet was quick with her left hook!'

But the publication of the book led Queen Elizabeth – later Queen Mother – to conclude that Crawfie had 'gone off her head'. She was cast adrift as if she had committed treason and neither the Queen nor the two Princesses ever spoke to her again. Her only crime had been to paint an affectionate and loyal portrait of a family to whom she had devoted a large part of her life – at considerable personal cost. But it was a crime for which she would never be forgiven.

Marion Crawford's own childhood had been a far cry from the world of palaces and castles that was to become so familiar. Born in a cottage near Kilmarnock in 1909, her father died when she was one year old. When her mother re-married, the family moved to Dunfermline, where Marion was educated. She always felt she had a vocation to teach, and imagined she would end up helping some of the poor and undernourished children she met during her training in Edinburgh. But fate intervened. No sooner was she qualified, than a network of acquaintances led her to the Duchess of York – and a plum job in the royal household. It was a bold step by the Duke and Duchess to employ someone as untested as Marion Crawford; not only was she inexperienced as a governess, she was also very young – at just twenty-four she was nine years the Duchess's junior. But this was part of her appeal; the Duke had unhappy memories of his elderly tutors and was determined that his girls should have someone with more energy.

Crawfie, as she was soon christened by her charges, found that her job description was fairly nebulous. Apart from running around with them, her chief instruction appears to have come from the children's grandfather, King George V, who appealed to her to 'teach Margaret and Lilibet to write a decent hand, that's all I ask you. Not one of my children can write properly.'

Those who knew her say Crawfie was a shy Scots girl, always extremely pleasant without being particularly interesting. No one questions her devotion to her two young charges, and the Princesses were equally devoted to her. Here, at last, was someone willing to join in their games.

The book paints an intimate portrait of life in the nursery: 'One of Lilibet's favourite games that went on for years was to harness me with a pair of red reins that had bells on them and off we would go, delivering groceries.'

It seems unsurprising that Lilibet – who in adult life is viewed as pretty buttoned up – was an extremely tidy child. Crawfie was struck by the immaculate condition of her thirty toy horses, each with its own saddle and bridle carefully polished by the girls themselves. At times the tidiness appeared to border on obsession, with Lilibet getting out of bed several times a night to check that her shoes were neatly lined up. It is with some relief that we learn that this serious child could have moments of rebellion – as she did during a desperately boring French lesson when she seized a silver inkpot and turned it upside down on her head. A predicament from which Crawfie had to rescue both the Princess and her French teacher.

Margaret, meanwhile, is portrayed as wilful and headstrong – spoiled by her parents but with a quick, bright mind. You get the impression that she was quite a handful for

Crawfie, but that her sometimes outrageous behaviour was refreshing in the confined world in which they all lived.

'There are so many things Margaret could have done with brilliance and distinction,' she writes. According to Crawfie, Lilibet was protective, even motherly, towards her younger sister.

'In her own intuitive fashion I think she saw ahead how later on Margaret was bound to be misrepresented and mis-understood.'

She did not, however, foresee that her own governess would become the Palace ogre who sold the family's secrets. Crawfie certainly gave no hint that she was intending to sell her story. Indeed, there is a piquant irony in the book as she recounts Lilibet's unhappiness about the publicity surrounding her engagement to Philip.

'The heart of a Princess is shy and as easily hurt as any other young girl's heart,' writes Crawfie. 'In time royalty grow accustomed and hardened to this prying into their private lives and make little of it. But not at nineteen. Not in love, deeply and passionately, for the first time.'

She concludes that royalty earn every penny they get for their loss of privacy.

So why, then, did Marion Crawford – so well-liked in royal circles, trusted by her employers and adored by the Princesses – decide to compromise that privacy, however sycophantically?

Several theories have been put forward, but the truth may never be known. One school of thought argues that Crawfie was seeking revenge because she was only made a 'Commander' of the Royal Victorian Order when she left the royal household, instead of the grander 'Dame Commander'.

There is, though, nothing that smacks of vengeance in this sympathetic and uncritical book. Another theory, unearthed in a television documentary fifty years after *The Little Princesses* was published, is more Machiavellian. It claims that Crawfie was the scapegoat for a botched PR campaign hatched by the Foreign Office and Queen Elizabeth (now Queen Mother) designed to improve the Royal Family's standing in the United States. According to this theory, the view was taken that a series of well-sourced articles in a top American magazine would do the Royal Family a power of good. Crawfie was allegedly told she could co-operate, as long as her name wasn't mentioned; but she failed to read the small print of the contract which allowed her to be named as the author.

Some of Crawfie's surviving contemporaries believe that there may indeed have been a misunderstanding that led her to believe she had clearance from Queen Elizabeth to help with some articles. But they also hold Crawfie's husband, George Buthlay, largely responsible for her downfall.

Given the demands of her job, it is astonishing that she found the time to meet and be wooed by anyone. The Royal Family are hard task-masters and expect their servants to give them undivided attention and loyalty. When she was thirty, however, Crawfie had to make a tough choice between her job and marriage. Her dedication to her employers was such that she didn't even mention her dilemma. Instead she told George Buthlay, an Aberdeen bank manager, that he would have to wait because war was looming and she would be needed more than ever at the Palace. It was only when Princess Elizabeth was on the brink of marriage, with Margaret almost eighteen and Crawfie herself thirty-eight, that she broached the subject with the Queen. The response was both sympathetic – acknowledging the sacrifice she had made – and selfish, as Crawfie recalls in her book:

'Does this mean you are going to leave us?' she (Queen Elizabeth) asked me. 'You must see, Crawfie, that it would not be at all convenient just now. A change at this stage for Margaret is not at all desirable.'

And so Crawfie carried on with her job for a couple more years, even after she was married and with her husband still in Scotland. It seems reasonable to accept that George felt some resentment about this, and had few qualms about encouraging his wife to cash in on the knowledge she had acquired during her long tenure at the heart of the Royal Family. Her account of life as a royal governess was first serialized in magazines in the States, but when the rights were bought by *Woman's Own*, her story became a front page sensation on both sides of the Atlantic. *The Little Princesses* followed shortly afterwards, netting Crawfie and George a total of more than £75,000 – an immense sum in those days.

The Royal Family instantly eliminated her from their lives.

According to friends, the Princesses were desperately hurt and disappointed that someone so close to them had betrayed their trust. The King and Queen were furious and had no hesitation in ostracizing her forever.

Crawfie retreated to Scotland, from where she began a new career as a journalist, with a column in *Woman's Own*. In fact there is some evidence that it was written for her, but the articles carried her name, along with news of royal and society events. Alarmingly, they all had to be written six weeks in advance because of the publishing deadlines for colour print. Eventually, the inevitable happened. In 1955, writing in the 16 June edition of the magazine, Crawfie gave a gushing description of the Trooping the Colour ceremony and went on to say how radiant the Queen had looked at Ascot. Unfortunately for her, neither of these events had taken place because of a rail strike. Her humiliation was complete and she was ridiculed in the newspapers.

When her husband died in 1977, Crawfie became more of a recluse. From her house on the road from Aberdeen to Balmoral, she could see the royal cars passing as the family came and went from their holidays. Not once did they call in to see her. Crawfie became lonely and depressed; she attempted suicide but was found by a neighbour. Often she would look through her most treasured possession, her box of mementoes of her life with the Royal Family: letters written to her by Queen Elizabeth during her tour of Canada in 1936, paintings and poems done for her by Lilibet and Margaret, photographs of the girls in the nursery. She could have sold them for a fortune; instead she left them to Lilibet in her will. When she died in 1988, the box of memories was taken into the Royal archive.

There is a consensus in royal circles that Crawfie was badly treated by her former employers. Most believe that her punishment outweighed her sin and that Queen Elizabeth and her daughters should have been magnanimous enough to forgive her. It must have been bewildering for the ageing governess to watch the shift in Palace policy while she remained exiled. What must she have thought when in 1969 Lilibet herself, with her husband and children, starred in a television documentary called *The Royal Family*? How insignificant her own revelations must have seemed as viewers were taken inside the Palace to share the family's life. The Queen's decision to allow cameras to follow her so closely is now seen as the start of a slippery slope that eventually led to Prince Charles admitting adultery on television and the Princess of Wales opening her heart to *Panorama*. How innocent, by comparison, does Crawfie's rose-tinted look at royal life now seem?

Much has changed in the half century since the book was written. The royal family is treated with less deference – partly because it has made it abundantly obvious that it is made up of fallible, vulnerable human beings just like the rest of us. They quarrel and have affairs, they divorce and re-marry; some are confused about their role, others are trying to live ordinary lives outside the royal circle. In the age of the telephoto lens, their privacy has been eroded. If Crawfie thought the young Princesses' right to a private life was compromised fifty years ago, how shocked would she have been by the daily newspaper revelations of recent decades accompanied by pictures of a topless Duchess, a Princess working out in the gym or leaked intimate phone conversations between royal lovers?

Looking back, there is so much more that Marion Crawford could have said, so many secrets she might have betrayed. If this is disloyalty, then it is a very caring and docile disloyalty. Whatever her reasons for writing *The Little Princesses*, Crawfie produced an important social document, taking us behind the Palace walls to enjoy a unique insight into the isolated childhood of the future Queen and her sister.

                                        JENNIE BOND

The
LITTLE
PRINCESSES

CHAPTER I

I Join the Household

I had always wanted to teach, but I had certainly never
intended to become a governess.

I was born on 5 June 1909, in the same house where my
mother, and her father before her, had been born – Woodside
Cottage, near Kilmarnock in Ayrshire. My father died when I
was a year old, and five years later – when I was six – my
mother remarried and we came to live in Dunfermline.

I studied at the Moray House Training College in
Edinburgh, and my training had taken me into the poorer
parts of the city. Here I saw a great deal of poverty, and had
to do with children who were not very bright because they
were undernourished. I was at that time very young, and I
became fired with a crusading spirit. I wanted to do something about the misery and unhappiness I saw all round me. I
wanted desperately to help. I always had a great sense of
vocation, and the feeling I had a job to do in life, and I had
quite made up my mind that this was what my job was to be.

Something else, however, was coming my way.

I had finished my exams, and gone home to rest.
Dunfermline is a small country town built on hills. Up to the
first world war it was the centre of the linen industry. Both the
Queen when she married, and Princess Elizabeth, were given
large chests of linen from Dunfermline.

It has a famous old abbey where the body of Robert the

3

Bruce is buried, and a lovely palace, now in ruins, which was the home of the early kings of Scotland. Once it was the capital of Scotland. Charles I was born there and the bed in which he was born is now part of a mantelpiece in nearby Broomhall, the home of the Earl and Countess of Elgin. Andrew Carnegie also was born in Dunfermline in a little humble cottage which remains quite untouched.

Broomhall is a square Georgian house, to the south looking on to the Forth; to the north one can see the lovely range of the Ochil Hills. It has a very large front hall, and round it are placed some of the Elgin marbles. It was old Lord Elgin who brought these over from Greece. As the family is directly descended from Robert the Bruce, his sword and helmet also hang in the hall. Both the helmet and sword are enormous, as he was an outsize man.

One morning I had a letter from Lady Elgin, who knew I had finished my training and had heard I was home on long leave, asking me if I would take her son Andrew, Lord Bruce, in history. He was a charming little boy of seven whom I already knew, and as I had nothing very definite to do when I wasn't studying myself, I took this on. What influenced me greatly was that I loved walking, and this post was within walking distance of my home, about three miles through shady woods and paths among the farms belonging to Lord Elgin, with occasional glimpses of the Forth through the trees.

As I sat writing the letter accepting Lady Elgin's offer, I little dreamed that here was one of those turning-points in life that we never do recognize when they first come along.

The Elgins were a charming family, very friendly and simple. Soon the three other Elgin children joined us – Lady Martha, Lady Jean and the Honourable Jamie. Presently I was running a small class at Broomhall, teaching other subjects besides history to four very nice children, and enjoying it thoroughly.

But I still thought of it as a temporary post, to tide me over until I could take up my real life-work.

The Elgins breakfasted early, about eight o'clock. I used to approach the french windows leading into the schoolroom to the strains of hymns and the tail-end of family prayers, and I would wait in the garden tactfully until these were finished. The children used to peep through their fingers during their devotions to watch for my coming.

Friends and relations were always dropping in and would join us for 'elevenses'. The grown-ups had coffee and the children a large glass of lemonade, rock cakes, and jam, while the domestic staff and garden workers would retire at the same time to still-room and stable for bread and cheese and cake on their own.

Most large country houses have a still-room. It is the housekeeper's domain, where all jams are made and stored, all fruit bottled, and light meals that need no cooking, like elevenses and afternoon tea, and after-dinner coffee, and so on, are prepared. It is really an extra pantry and store-room. The linen is mended there, and peaches and fruit are stored. It probably comes from the old days when ales were brewed and home-made wines made.

Lady Rose Leveson-Gower came about this time to Rosyth with her husband, the Admiral, who was stationed there. Rosyth is on the banks of the Forth not far from Broomhall. I was asked if I would take their little girl, Mary, who was rather delicate, for a short session every day.

So now in the good weather, which is not so infrequent in Scotland as some people suppose, I had a really fine day's walking. I would do the three miles to Admiralty House from Broomhall when I had finished my class there. Then when the day's work was over, I would walk home again.

It seemed to me then that this was just a pleasant interlude, a temporary arrangement to fill in the time between one course of study and the next. I intended, as soon as my present pupils were ready for school, to return to my first love, which was child psychology. I spent my evenings reading and studying for this very happily. I was twenty-two. At twenty-two one has the illusion of there being lots of time.

Meanwhile, Fate was marching up on me in the way Fate has. There came one lovely morning when I walked as usual through the gardens of Admiralty House for my session with Mary. The gardens were very charming. Terraces ran down to the River Forth, overlooking a bay called Saint Margaret's Hope, after Margaret, sister of Edgar Atheling, the Saxon King. She married Malcolm Canmore, King of Scotland. The chroniclers say she was learned and pious, and a keen politician. She did a lot to bring English ways and customs up to Scotland, and it was here she is supposed to have landed when she came north. I always took this part of my walk slowly.

   Lady Rose told me that her sister, the Duchess of York, was coming to see her with the Duke, and that she wanted me to meet them. There were always visitors coming and going, and we were seldom alone for our elevenses. As I crossed the lawn I remember there came over me an eerie feeling that someone was watching me. It made me look up toward the house. Then it was I saw there was a face at the window, and for the first time I met that long cool stare I was later to come to know so well.

Lady Rose's sister, the pretty little Duchess of York, and her young husband, the Duke, were the visitors. I was introduced to them as usual, and we all ate our buns and drank our coffee before Mary and I went off to work. I was quite enchanted, as people always were, by the little Duchess. She was petite, as her daughter Margaret is today. She had the nicest, easiest, most friendly of manners, and a merry laugh. It was impossible to feel shy in her presence. She was beautifully dressed in blue. There was nothing alarmingly fashionable about her. Her hair was done in a way that suited her admirably, with a little fringe over her forehead.

She sat on the window ledge. The blue of her dress, I remember, exactly matched the sky behind her that morning and the blue of her eyes. I particularly noticed her lovely string of pearls. She did not wear ear-rings then. Her hands and feet were tiny. My whole impression was of someone small and quite perfect.

The Duke was extraordinarily handsome, but I recall thinking he did not look very strong. He was slight, and looked like a boy of eighteen, though he was considerably older than I. He had a diffident manner and a slight impediment in his speech that was not so much of a stutter in the ordinary sense, as a slight nervous constriction of the throat, I thought. It was obvious that they were devoted to each other and very much in love, and I remember thinking they looked just as a Duke and a Duchess ought to look, but often don't.

No word of any kind was said, or any hint given me of what was coming. Two weeks later Lady Rose told me that the Duke and Duchess had talked the matter over and had decided to ask me to undertake the education of their daughters, Princesses Elizabeth and Margaret Rose, then aged five and two. They fully realized, Lady Rose said, that there might be some opposition to this arrangement in certain quarters because of my youth, but both the Duke and Duchess were anxious that the little girls should have someone with them young enough to enjoy playing games and running about with them. The Duke, I gathered, had throughout his own childhood been hampered by somewhat immobile pastors and masters. He wanted someone energetic with his children, and had been impressed by the amount of walking I did!

I told Lady Rose that, if I accepted the post, it would mean that I would not be able to go on with what I had intended to be my life's work – child psychology; but that it was a great honour and I should like some time to consider the matter.

In two weeks' time, I wrote to the Duchess saying how honoured I was to have been asked to undertake the education of the Princesses, and I suggested that I should take up the work for a trial period during which I would be able to determine whether it would be easy for me to become reconciled to the idea of leaving Scotland and my intended career, and living permanently with other people.

The Duchess wrote me a charming, friendly little letter: 'Why not come for a month and see how you like us and how we like you?'

That seemed a sensible arrangement. It was fixed that I would go to them at Royal Lodge, Windsor, just before Easter.

I remember feeling distinctly apprehensive on the long journey south from Scotland. I had led the quiet open-air life of a Scottish girl. I knew nothing whatever about court etiquette. I was a little scared, doubtful whether I was doing the right thing. All the children I had had to do with at the Elgins' and the Leveson-Gowers' had been pleasant and amenable, and easy to deal with. It was a couple of very spoiled and difficult little people I somehow visualized as I travelled south, for already the papers had produced odd stories about these royal children. I was more than convinced that my month's trial would stop at the end of the month, and that I should soon be home again.

From the train I had my first glimpse of Windsor Castle. I saw it first in the gathering shadows of a spring twilight. It looms up suddenly, topping the whole countryside, a fantastic mass of turrets and battlements and towers. It is incredibly old.

The stone circuit wall was built by William the Conqueror. Henry III contributed the first complete round tower in 1272. Though George IV rebuilt so much of the Castle, there is still beneath it a sinister labyrinth of dungeons, most with their own sinister stories, some with pathetic little scratches made on the walls by prisoners of other days.

Little I dreamed then how well I was to come to know the place, or how one day I, too, would be hidden away there, as securely and as secretly as any political prisoner waiting to be relieved of her head.

A tall, handsome, courteous man met me on the steps of the front door of Royal Lodge. This was Ainslie, the butler, who was to become one of my fast friends. He is now steward at Buckingham Palace. His beautiful manners alone were enough to take him a very long way.

The Duke and Duchess, he told me, had had to go to London and would not be back until later. But Her Royal Highness had had special permission to sit up for me, so would I go straight up to the nurseries, as Mrs Knight did not like the Princess to be kept up late.

Mrs Knight was called by everyone Alah, probably a childish version of her Christian name which was Clara. She had been nanny to the Duchess and her brother David as babies. She was a tall, noble-looking woman, born in Hertfordshire. She was not, like so many of the royal attendants, a Scotswoman. She was what every good nurse ought to be – calm and kind, exuding that comfortable air of infallibility and security so necessary to the welfare of the young.

English nursery tradition is dying out now, along with other admirable institutions that have provided some of our finest citizens. The nursery was a world in miniature, a state within a state. The head of the state was the nurse, usually called Nanny or Nana. It was into her kind arms that the latest baby was handed when the monthly nurse departed. It

was she who had the entire upbringing and training of him
until the cruel years when school came and he was torn from
her, at eight.

She would have a nursemaid to help her and wait on her,
who in turn would be training to be a nanny herself. In the
more important households there would be a footman and a
housemaid told off to wait on the nurseries as well.

The system was open to abuse when the nurse in charge
was a tyrant, as she sometimes was. But mostly these were
dedicated women as surely as nuns are. They had a real vocation, and it is impossible to convey to anyone who has not
known it the comfort and serenity those old-fashioned nurseries had.

They would mostly be upstairs, shut off on the sunny side
of the house. A fire usually burned behind a high wire fire-
guard on which baby clothes would always be airing, and in
front of which the latest baby was bathed. There was always
a rocking-chair in which Nanny would rock sufferers from
bumps or private sorrows back to serenity. She was always
there, a shoulder to weep on, a bosom to fall asleep on. She
would sit at evening in the rocker, the children around her on
the hearthrug, mending or knitting and telling stories of 'when
Mummie was a little girl'.

For nannies were handed on. When one family grew up she
would go with them, and be a nanny to their babies. When a
family fell on evil days and all the rest had fled, Nanny often
remained even when no wages could be paid her, one of the
family, taking the rough with the smooth, inaugurating in a
different and smaller place that atmosphere of comfort and
warmth, and the smell of hot flannel and camphorated oil
which those of us who remember those other days can never
forget.

The matron of a small boys' school once told me that on the
first nights of school terms, most of her homesick little boys

wept, not for Mummie but for their nanny. She was much more than a paid servant; she was their childhood.

Here and there in England these devoted women are still to be found, the sweet sound core of many a home. But they are dying out fast. This was another world, shattered by the bombs!

Alah awaited me with that mixture of reserve and apprehension felt by all nannies when the governess is introduced. I like to remember that in all my years at 145 Piccadilly, London, and later at Buckingham Palace, Alah and I remained good friends; and if on her side the neutrality was sometimes armed to the teeth, I was always very careful not to tread on her toes.

Alah had entire charge in those days of the children's out-of-school lives – their health, their baths, their clothes – while I had them from nine to six. She had to help her an under-nurse and a nursemaid. These two girls are there still – Margaret MacDonald and Ruby MacDonald, two sisters, who have become the personal maids and friends of two sisters.

The night nursery was decorated in pink and fawn, the Duchess's favourite colour scheme. A small figure with a mop of curls sat up in bed. She wore a nightie with a design of small pink roses on it. She had tied the cords of her dressing gown to the knobs of the old-fashioned bed, and was busy driving her team.

That was my first glimpse of Princess Elizabeth.

'This is Miss Crawford,' said Alah, in her stern way.

The little girl said, 'How do you do.' She then gave me a long, comprehensive look I had seen once before, and went on, 'Why have you no hair?'

I pulled off my hat to show her. 'I have enough to go on with,' I said. 'It's an Eton crop.'

She picked up her reins again.

'Do you usually drive in bed?' I asked.

'I mostly go once or twice round the park before I go to sleep, you know,' she said. 'It exercises my horses.' She navigated a dangerous and difficult corner, and went on, 'Are you going to stay with us?'

'For a little while, anyway,' I replied.

'Will you play with us tomorrow? Will you come to the Little House with us?' she asked eagerly. Alah had by now unhitched the team, and laid her flat. She allowed herself to be tucked away like a small doll. 'Good night. See you tomorrow,' she said to me.

Royal Lodge was originally a shooting-box built by George IV. The original part left is a large drawing room, which is called the saloon, and an octagon room and the wine cellar underneath. It has been painted pink because the Queen had spent happy years of her childhood in a pink house and had kept a great affection for it. Royal Lodge is quite the most up-to-date of the royal establishments. It is plain and simple, and might have been any country gentleman's home.

I had dinner alone on a tray in a pleasant sitting room upholstered in chintz. To my horror, a large fire was burning there. After Scotland, the south seemed to be almost unbearably warm and close, and I could hardly breathe. Upstairs a cheerful housemaid had done some of my unpacking for me. The schoolroom on the second floor looked out over the gardens, and the whole atmosphere of the comfortable, unpretentious pink house was homelike and informal. Some of my apprehension began to disappear.

The Duchess came in later that evening, wearing her going-out clothes, having just come down from London, twenty-five miles away. She had a sort of sheen or brightness about her in those days. She was thirty-one, and her way of speaking was the easy, friendly one of any girl in her own home speaking to another girl who was far from home and might be a little homesick and needed to be put at her ease. She wore as usual blue, and I still thought her one of the loveliest people I had ever seen.

She had a gentle, kindly manner of looking at you. Her eyes were her most outstanding feature, very blue, very sympathetic, and she looked incredibly youthful. The old enchantment I had felt up north still held me. When she said, 'I do hope you will be happy here, and like us,' I replied, 'I am sure I shall.' And I meant every word of it.

CHAPTER II

Royal Lodge and
145 Piccadilly

BREAKFAST was brought to me in my room on my first morning at Royal Lodge. But before that I had been conscious of shrieks of laughter close at hand. An unholy din filled the air for some time. This I learned was the usual procedure. The little girls were having their morning session in their parents' room. No matter how busy the day, how early the start that had to be made, each morning began with high jinks in their parents' bedroom. Both children had sweet, bell-like voices, pleasant to hear, and it was difficult not to join in the laughter, even at a distance. It was somewhere around ten o'clock before they went off to Alah.

From the time of my arrival, Lilibet came down to me. She had given herself this name when she found 'Elizabeth' rather difficult to get round, and it had stuck to her ever since.

The first morning she showed me the Little House. The Little House was a present from the people of Wales. For many years it was the Princesses' favourite toy. It still stands in the grounds of Royal Lodge, a nicely matured garden now growing up round it, waiting for its next tenant. Princess Elizabeth will probably have it moved one day to her country home for her own children.

14

It had its name neatly printed above the door, 'Y Bwthyn Bach', or The Little House. Welsh thatchers came up from time to time to attend to the roof. It is rethatched every three or four years.

Later it became impossible to get Welsh thatchers. The art has died out there. So English thatchers came.

The Little House was built to scale for children, and a bit on the small side for me. I could get round by going on my knees. There was one place on the landing where I could stand upright, all five feet seven of me.

The house is complete in every detail, with blue chintz curtains at windows which really open, with plumbing that works and lights that go on and off. What especially enchanted me that first day was the small oil-painting of the Duchess that hung over the little mantelshelf in the drawing-room. It was done to scale by Miss Sybil Charlotte Williams, a Welsh artist, and it is one of the best likenesses I have seen of the Duchess as she was then, with her sweet expression and lovely colouring, and the individual, and at that time not fashionable, way she did her hair.

There was a radio that worked, an oak dresser with a complete outfit of china, buttercup yellow, and an outfit of linen with the initial 'E' and a crown. I opened a drawer and found an insurance policy such as must be carried by every prudent housewife. There was also a radio-set licence. There was in the bookshelves a complete set of Beatrix Potter's books. One in Welsh!

The kitchen of the Little House had every possible utensil and cooking pot, and an outfit of stores of canned goods. All in miniature. There were brooms and pans, baking powder and flour, and there was even a miniature packet of Epsom salts!

I found the whole place quite enchanting, and at that time I remember being immensely impressed by the wonderful order there. I thought without any doubt someone came down from time to time to clean and dust and keep the place in order. But not a bit of it. The little girls looked after it themselves, and probably learned in doing so more than any domestic-science school could have taught them. For which, grateful thanks to the people of Wales.

The children copied, as children always will, what they saw around them. Lilibet was then rising six, but she put away the blankets and linen and wrapped up the silver in newspaper 'to prevent it getting tarnished, Crawfie', as she told me some time later, whenever we went to London. The furniture was covered with dust sheets, just as the staff did in the main house when we went away. Children reflect what they see going on around them. This sense of order was, I found, very strong in the family of my new employers.

The Duke and the Duchess had their bedrooms on the ground floor. It was an odd arrangement, because bedrooms are usually upstairs, but they seemed to like it. The windows were fitted with grilles, and the house was full of burglarproof gadgets.

The large double bed in the Duchess's room had blue silk covers and lemon pleatings. The carpets are of the Queen's favourite colour to this day – misty blue. There was a large kidney-shaped dressing-table, glass-topped, everything on it kept beautifully tidy. The furniture and cupboards were all very simple and unadorned, of white apple wood. The only real luxury was that the cupboards lit up inside when you opened them.

The Duke's room always reminded me of a cabin on a ship. Wherever he was, he managed to give that air to it. A blue-green draped bed, very hard-looking, a solid dressing-table that itself had a nautical air, and one bookcase were all the furniture he had in it in those days. Here, too, everything was laid out very precisely and neatly, as if for a parade inspection.

Later, when they were engulfed in Buckingham Palace with its marble and crystal, its plush and gilt, much the same atmosphere hung over their two rooms. The King's was always immaculately tidy and vaguely nautical, the Queen's always fragrant with flowers. The perfume of certain flowers always brings her back to me. Especially roses.

Lilibet and I started lessons at nine-thirty in the morning, when she had finished her breakfast with Alah in the nursery. I breakfasted in my sitting room, alone. It looked out on to the gardens. There are incredible numbers of rare birds at Royal Lodge. It is hard to believe it is only twenty-five miles from London. Later on we fixed up a bird-bell and a bird-table. The smaller birds would come and ring the bell to get the food out.

Though not yet six, Lilibet had begun her riding lessons with Owen the groom and she liked me to come and watch her. Her first canter was a great day. I used to walk with the dogs, and it was very pretty to hear her small bell-like voice through the trees talking to Owen about burs, galls, and girths.

I began to love the beauty of the peaceful daily life we had. Lunch was great fun. We four had this together. Margaret came down at the end of the meal. It was a great delight to see her opening the door gently and pushing her small fat face round it.

The Duke always asked her what she had had for lunch, and we had wonderful descriptions. She would hold out her hand and her father would put a spoonful of coffee sugar into it. Lilibet also had a great weakness for this, which was the good old-fashioned barley sugar known as 'Rock of Ages'.

The two little girls had their own way of dealing with their sugar. Margaret kept the whole lot in her small hot hand and pushed it into her mouth. Lilibet, however, carefully sorted hers out on the table, large and small pieces together, and then ate it very daintily and methodically.

The Royal Family in those days did not use white table-cloths. They dined at a glass-topped table, with dinner mats, square, made of parchment. One set had birds, and another set flowers painted on them.

It is interesting to note how the coffee-sugar habit hung on. Years later, when both girls were quite big, and we were at Windsor Castle during the war, the coffee sugar would be ceremoniously handed to both the Princesses by the footman, and they would each take a handful though they never drank coffee.

One day I learned that King George V and Queen Mary were coming to tea. This was quite an unusual occurrence. The Royal Family visit one another very rarely and seldom all meet *en masse* unless there is a coronation, christening, wedding, or funeral in their midst. There is little dropping in and out on casual visits, though numerous notes are exchanged.

So this was quite an event. No one said anything to me, but I had a shrewd suspicion they were coming down to have a look at me. I sensed that Their Majesties had belonged to that circle who disapproved of my appointment and considered me much too young.

I mentioned this to the Duchess, who laughed and agreed. 'There is an idea going round that someone older would have been a better choice, but the Duke and I don't think so. We want our children to have a happy childhood which they can always look back on,' she said.

The ordeal drew nearer. I was not much good at curtsying in those days. It is an acquired art, as one is apt to topple. There is nothing more beautiful than a curtsy that is gracefully done; it is an act of homage to the sovereign. It takes practice. I went round the gardens practising assiduously to a British oak. Only later did I realize how suitable was my choice.

Afternoon came. The children remained indoors to welcome their grandparents. I expected they would all come out into the garden together, and that I would be ceremoniously presented.

Not a bit of it. Over the lawn by themselves came King George and Queen Mary, a truly imposing couple. The King was then in his late sixties, a very imposing figure. Queen Mary looked taller than he because she had such a magnificent carriage.

There was no one to present me. Queen Mary stopped, leaned on her ever-present folded silk umbrella, and said, 'You are Miss Crawford.'

I made my deepest curtsy, one to each of them, the King first. They looked me over with that long, now-becoming-familiar searching look. I remember I had an almost irresistible desire to say, 'Please, will I do?'

Apparently I would. Queen Mary said nothing at all, but she smiled at me. King George grunted and prodded the ground with his stick. At first acquaintance he was rather disconcerting. He had a loud, booming voice, rather terrifying to children and young ladies who did not know him. After a moment he said:

'For goodness' sake, teach Margaret and Lilibet to write a decent hand, that's all I ask you. Not one of my children can write properly. They all do it exactly the same way.'

'I like a hand with some character in it,' he added, and walked away.

They overawed me a little at the time. Later I was to have a very great love and affection for Queen Mary. There were many times when I went to her in trouble. She was always a rock of strength and wisdom to me, someone I could go to in moments of doubt and difficulty. There were to be plenty of both.

Margaret was an enchanting, doll-like child, still in the nursery. She was Alah's sole charge, and I saw little of her at first. She was the baby everyone loves at sight, but from the very beginning I had a feeling about Lilibet that she was 'special'. I had met many children of all sorts in my time, but never one with so much character at so young an age, and it was not long before I had made up my mind that should the job be offered to me permanently, I would accept it.

It was my first experience with royalty's economy in words, which I was to come to know so well. My month became five weeks, five weeks was rapidly turning into six, and still no word was said either of my staying or departing. In the end I went to the Duchess, who was a little surprised I had needed to ask. Both she and the Duke had thought I would somehow realize, without any unnecessary talk, that they thought I would do.

'But of course you must stay,' she said, as if the whole affair had been settled long ago. Perhaps it is having people always on hand to attend to detail and staff work that engenders this rather vague frame of mind among royalty that is often amusing, but occasionally somewhat disconcerting.

I told the Duchess I must go home first to set my own affairs in order, consult my mother, and pack my belongings. I reminded her that originally I had come down for only a month. The Duchess seemed surprised.

Back in Dunfermline, I had to get together what was, for me, a trousseau of clothes suitable to my new life. This was quite a problem and a great expense, but thanks to a wonderful mother who was clever with her needle, I went south again ready for any royal occasion. As it turned out, life at 145 Piccadilly was very quiet and the demands on my wardrobe were not so severe a strain as they were to become later, when the family moved to Buckingham Palace. Then dress was to become a problem, and I had to spend most of my salary on clothes. One of my most successful evening frocks, I remember, was made out of some blue tapestry that had originally been intended for curtains in my bedroom at home.

In the autumn I returned to the Royal Family, a permanent member of the ducal household at 145 Piccadilly.

No. 145 was a tall, narrow house, just beyond Hyde Park Corner, two doors from the house that once belonged to the Duke of Wellington. St George's Hospital is almost opposite. Its lit windows used to shine out at us all through the night. The house had an enclosed space, known as Hamilton Gardens, behind it. A gate led out from there into Hyde Park. During the war, the railings were removed, and the once well-kept garden is a sad sight of dilapidation now.

It was a homelike and unpretentious household I found myself in. It was a home the centre of which was undoubtedly the nurseries. They were on the top floor, comfortable, sunny rooms that opened on to a landing beneath a big glass dome. Round the dome stood some thirty-odd toy horses about a foot high on wheels.

'That's where we stable them,' Lilibet explained, and she showed me that each horse there had its own saddle and bridle, which were kept immaculate and polished by the little girls themselves. Over the years the collection had accumulated, for when in doubt as to Christmas and birthday presents, it was always safe to send another horse.

Stable routine was strictly observed. Each horse had its saddle removed nightly and was duly fed and watered. No matter what else might be going on, this was a must-be-done chore. The obsession for toy horses lasted unbroken until real horses became important some years later, and even then the old friends were not forgotten. They stood in a row along one of the corridors at Buckingham Palace, their grooming basket at the end of the row, for many a year.

One of Lilibet's favourite games that went on for years was to harness me with a pair of red reins that had bells on them, and off we would go, delivering groceries. I would be gentled, patted, given my nosebag, and jerked to a standstill, while

Lilibet, at imaginary houses, delivered imaginary groceries, and held long and intimate conversations with her make-believe customers.

Sometimes she would whisper to me, 'Crawfie, you must pretend to be impatient. Paw the ground a bit.' So I would paw.

Frosty mornings were wonderful, for then my breath came in clouds, 'just like a proper horse,' said Lilibet contentedly. Or she herself would be the horse, prancing around, sidling up to me, nosing in my pockets for sugar, making convincing little whinnying noises.

Besides the toy horses there were other four-legged friends in the world outside. A brewer's dray with a fine pair often pulled up in Piccadilly just below, stopped by the traffic lights. There they would stand, steaming, on winter nights. The little girls, their faces pressed to the nursery window, would watch for them fondly, anxious if they were late. On wet streets anything might happen to big dray horses. And many a weary little pony trotting home at the end of the day in its coster's cart little dreamed of the wealth of royal sympathy it roused, from that upper window.

From another side of the house we could see the riding schools going along Rotten Row. At the end of the track they would turn, and start off again, the same horse appearing several times a day with different riders.

'If I am ever Queen,' said Lilibet firmly, 'I shall make a law that there must be no riding on Sundays. Horses should have a rest too. And I shan't let anyone dock their pony's tail.'

The house at 145 Piccadilly was neither large nor splendid. It might have been the home of any moderately well-to-do young couple starting married life. My bedroom, on the fourth floor, was the only spare room. Lilibet's room was next door. There was no official schoolroom. We did lessons in a pleasant little boudoir belonging to the Duchess, off the big drawing room. I have never known a house with a nicer atmosphere. The children's bell-like voices floated down the well of the dome, calling to each other, or fondly addressing their horses. It has often seemed to me since that in those days we lived in an ivory tower, removed from the real world. The Duke and Duchess were so young, and so much in love. They took great delight in each other and in their children. Looking back on it, it often seems to me as though while we were there the season was always spring.

The morning session in their parents' room began the day at about nine o'clock, as it always continued to do right up to the morning of Princess Elizabeth's marriage. The children's bath hour and bedtime, again with the parents, ended the day. Nothing was ever allowed to stand in the way of these family sessions.

Lessons now began for Lilibet. She was rising six. I found she could already read; her mother had taught her, at five. She proved an immensely interesting child to teach, with a high IQ, and from the start there was always about her a certain amenability, a reasonableness rare in anyone so very young. She was quick at picking anything up, and one never had to do a lot of explaining to her. I found later on the same bright quickness of mind in Margaret, who knew the look of words and could recognize them by eye long before she could spell them or read properly, but she did not make such rapid progress as Lilibet, and read much later.

As our first reader we took Barrie's *Peter Pan in Kensington Gardens*, a book both children were very fond of. They also began to read the *Children's Newspaper*, an excellent little publication setting out current happenings in simple language. I believe it is delivered to them still. They took to newspaper reading very early, and like most children delighted in the comic strips, both English and American. Presently, when Lilibet was older, part of her daily lesson was reading *The*

Times. But in the earlier days the horizon was rather blocked by 'Pip, Squeak, and Wilfred', 'Mutt and Jeff', and 'Li'l Abner'.

The children could not have been more simply dressed. They wore cotton frocks, mostly blue with a flower pattern, and little cardigan coats to match when it was cool. Blue of a certain misty shade was always the Duchess's favourite colour, and it happened to be mine as well. More than once on coming down to lunch I found we were all dressed in the same colour. After that I tactfully adopted brown.

Lilibet had a passion for cherry red, and a red coat she was particularly attached to. Margaret was still a baby of two, but rather wistful about it. For a time she was kept back, and this led to a rumour going around that there was something wrong with her. One school of thought had it that she was deaf and dumb, a notion not without its humour to those who knew her.

I fancy Alah was to blame for this. Alah, like all fond nannies, longed to keep one baby in the nursery and, as no new one was forthcoming, clung on to Margaret so that the long-suffering child was penned in a pram long after she pined to run about with us in the gardens, and was fed by hand when in reality she had done with such childish things.

I don't think Alah ever quite approved of the simple lives the little girls led, or their almost severe wardrobes. She was a great deal more regal than her youthful master and mistress; and to her way of thinking, little princesses should be little princesses always. Even in their baths. She never quite approved of their plain tweed coats, business-like berets and stout walking shoes. Only at their rare parties did Alah come into her own and produce two dear little figures like dolls, all organdie frills and ribbons and bows.

The little girls had each a necklace of coral and real pearls made from a string of their mother's broken up for them.

These they wore for parties, and they were very proud of them. Otherwise they had no jewellery except toy brooches and beads strung by themselves.

Margaret took a warm interest in her toilettes from an early age. I remember I used to tease her later on and tell her I was sure that the first thing she did when she was old enough to sit up was to tie a bow in her hair.

Lilibet never cared a fig. She wore what she was told without argument, apart from a certain long, drab mackintosh, which she loathed. She was never happier than when she was thoroughly busy and rather grubby. Until I came, she had never been allowed to get dirty. Life had consisted of drives in the park, or quiet ladylike games in Hamilton Gardens, keeping to the paths; or leisurely drives around London in an open victoria, waving graciously to people when Alah told her to do so.

I started a few innovations. We played Red Indians among the shrubberies. London bushes make fine cover for ambushes, but they are extremely smutty. We ran a horse market with their assorted steeds. We played hide-and-seek, and sardines – a form of hide-and-seek in which you do not catch your man, but creep in beside him when you have found him. The next person who finds these two creeps in also until there is only one disconsolate seeker left, the loser. When the original hiding-place is a small one under a rhodo-dendron bush, the resulting jam there resembles the inside of a tin of sardines.

Other residents in Hamilton Place had keys to the gardens. They came and went. The little girls had names for all of them. I was told of a Miss Woggs and a Mrs Happy. I did not rec-ognize for some little time that these were the names of their dogs. It was only when Lilibet pointed out a Mr Schipperke to me that the truth dawned on me. Mr Schipperke's schip-perke died one day and was buried in the gardens. Lilibet was shattered by this, and wove a small wreath of poppies for the grave. It happened on Poppy Day.

So engrossed in their games were the children that they never noticed the faces so often lined up at the railings that gave on to the park, watching them. It was a thing that at first I found immensely trying. In time I, too, became hardened to these ever-present onlookers at every possible occasion, and came to notice them no more than the children did themselves.

From time to time elaborate toys would arrive as presents. All kinds of people were apt to send the little girls things, but at this time no presents were ever accepted from people they did not know, and the gifts would be packed up again and returned with a kind note.

The children much preferred simple and inexpensive things they got for themselves. I had a long table made, and Lilibet and I collected a large farm, buying most of the pieces at Woolworth's. She went through a phase of being very farm-minded, and at one time used to say that when she grew up she would marry a farmer. 'I shall have lots of cows, horses, and children,' she told me gravely.

There had been some little difficulty in deciding what the children were to call me. Lilibet was accustomed to call the various ladies-in-waiting by their Christian names. She asked me mine, and announced she would call me Marion. This did not seem to be particularly good for discipline, and I had not quite made up my mind what to do about it when the matter solved itself conveniently one day. We were playing ball together, Lilibet and I, and she dropped catch after catch. After about six dropped balls she said suddenly, despairingly, 'Oh, Crawfie!' Then she paused and looked at me, pleased with herself. 'There!' she said. 'That's what I'll call you.'

So 'Crawfie' it was and still is, to a great many other people now besides the children at the Palace.

Princess Elizabeth and Princess Margaret in 1932

Princess Elizabeth and her baby sister out for a ride with Mrs Knight (Alah)

A birthday portrait of Princess Margaret, aged two

A photograph of the little Princesses taken in 1932 at the St Paul's Walden home of their grandparents, Lord and Lady Strathmore

*The children play together in the nursery
that was once their mother's,
at St Paul's Walden*

*The Princesses, with Alah, arrive for a
holiday visit to Birkhall*

Princess Margaret, aged three

High jinks at Abergeldie Castle Fête
in 1933. Princess Elizabeth has a
tug-of-war while Princess Margaret
engages in a private tussle
with a tent-rope

Princess Margaret sells white heather to
a visitor at the Fête

The Duchess of York arriving with her daughters at Glamis Station

Princess Elizabeth stands proudly on the doorstep of the Little House, presented to her by the people of Wales

The Princess 'at home' with two of her pets

Princess Elizabeth riding in Windsor Great Park with her favourite groom, Mr Owen

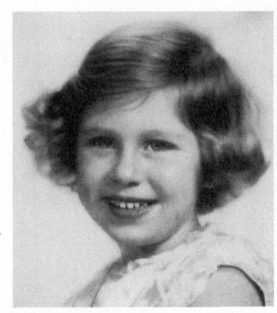

*A happy photograph of
Princess Margaret
when she was four years old*

Princess Margaret's sparkling, playful nature is well captured in this little-known photograph

*The Duke and Duchess and their daughters pose with their dogs
in the grounds of Royal Lodge, Windsor*

*Dogs have always been a prominent feature of the royal household.
Here, the Princesses coax some of their playmates to sit for the camera*

Princess Elizabeth and Dookie take a rest together after a game in Hamilton Gardens

The Princesses inspect the docks and shipping at the model village of Bekonscot in Buckinghamshire

A few of the horses from the Piccadilly 'stable'

With critical eyes, the Princesses watch an inspection of the Yeoman of the Guard by the Duke of Connaught at St James's Palace

No. 145 Piccadilly, until 1937 the London home of the Duke and Duchess of York

A charming portrait of the Princesses and their mother taken in December 1936

Princess Elizabeth rides with her parents and King George V to Crathie Church, near Balmoral

The royal children join in the fun at the Master of Carnegie's sixth birthday party

Both the Princesses were very keen horsewomen and greatly enjoyed riding with their father in Windsor Great Park. Here they are seen returning from an afternoon's outing

Princess Elizabeth makes friends with an elephant during a visit to London Zoo

A game of 'horses and carts' with Margaret Elphinstone.
With her left foot Princess Elizabeth impatiently 'paws' the ground

Princess Margaret clutches her ticket firmly as, with Lady Helen Graham and Miss Crawford,
the Princesses arrive at the underground station on an unofficial visit to the Great Russell Street
headquarters of the YWCA

Glamis Castle

*At Royal Lodge, Windsor. The
Princesses are about to put in
some work on their garden plots*

They were always good at names for both real and imaginary people, and it was difficult till you got to know them all to separate fancy from fact. Margaret had an imaginary crony called Cousin Halifax of whom she made every use when she wanted to be tiresome. Nothing was Margaret's fault; Cousin Halifax was entirely to blame for tasks undone and things forgotten. 'I was busy with Cousin Halifax,' she would say haughtily, watching me out of the corner of her eye to see if I looked like swallowing that excuse.

The Duke often came out and joined us in the gardens in the morning break. Sometimes he played hide-and-seek with us. He was the fastest runner I have ever known. I can still see him putting on an immense spurt round the statue of Byron which stood in the gardens there and came in very handy for us as 'home'. In those early days the Duke of York, with his boyish appearance and delicate look, was not considered to be a particularly important person in the family. He had no official position other than that of royal Prince. He was generally helpful, ready to do anything his father, King George, wanted him to do. He opened bazaars and took his turn at inspections. His own pet interest was the Duke of York Camps which he inaugurated and attended every year, and greatly enjoyed.

These camps brought together public-school boys and poor boys from the East End of London, and the Duke himself would go down every year and go under canvas with them, and sit round and sing campfire songs, many of them with actions which he would come back and teach to Lilibet and Margaret. A great favourite was 'Under the Spreading Chestnut Tree'. One year the camp was held at Abergeldie, which is close to Balmoral. The children loved that, as they were able to go to the camp each day and join in the fun.

The centre of interest in the family then was golden-haired Uncle David, the apple of his mother's eye and England's future King. It did not seem then even remotely likely that the tall, slim young man with the shy manner and the impediment in his speech which made him dislike publicity of any kind, would ever mean much to England. He was the domesticated one, the happily married one whose whole life revolved round his pretty wife and his delightful little girls.

Lilibet was now promoted to lunch downstairs. We had it with the Duke and the Duchess, who also, when they were at home during the morning, had joined us for elevenses. A special milk pudding always arrived for Lilibet. She used to eye it mournfully as it was borne in, refused by the Duke and Duchess, and by me, and firmly served to herself.

'It's good for you,' said the Duchess.

'If it's so good for me, I think Crawfie ought to have some too. It's good for her also,' said Lilibet one day, eyeing me firmly. So the dish was handed back to me, and I had to take some too.

As far as education was concerned, the Duke and Duchess reposed great confidence in me, leaving much to my judgement. No one ever had employers who interfered so little.

Later I came to feel this was a very great responsibility, and it worried me a lot. I was to find here a wonderful ally in Queen Mary, whose advice and suggestions were always immensely practical and helpful. Perhaps it was generally conceded in those days that the education of two not very important little girls did not matter a great deal. Nothing then seemed less likely than that they would ever have to play any very important role in life.

I had often the feeling that the Duke and Duchess, most happy in their own married life, were not over concerned with the higher education of their daughters. They wanted most for them a really happy childhood, with lots of pleasant memories stored up against the days that might come and, later, happy marriages.

Presently Margaret clambered out of her pram with resolution, and there was nothing more Alah could do about it. No new baby had appeared – I sometimes thought this was a sorrow – and the pram was sadly put away where it remained in purdah for some years together with the baby basket, the trimmed-up crib, and the hoosh-mi dish.

'Hoosh-mi' is a pleasant word made up by Margaret for the nursery mixture of chopped meat, potato, and gravy, all 'hoosh-mied' up together and spoon-fed to its victim. Later the word was to become part of the schoolroom vocabulary, and a mix of any kind was always known as a hoosh-mi.

Now, after finishing her lunch upstairs, Margaret would join us in the dining room. She always went straight to her father's side, climbed up on his knee, and clamoured for soda water. 'Windy water' she called it. The Duke always made the same remark: 'You can't like it!' She would nod, and say, 'Oh, yes I do. It crackles in my nose.' She wore cotton frocks with little pockets; in one there was always a handkerchief, usually with an embroidered hunting scene in the corner, and a tiny watch, with which she always pretended solemnly to tell the time.

As soon as Margaret came out to join us in our games in Hamilton Gardens, the rumour that she was either deaf or dumb died a natural death, for the air resounded with her pretty, dear little voice crying, 'Wait for me, Lilibet ... Wait for me!' which was her signature tune for many years to come.

The little girls were good friends, though both had fiery tempers and from time to time would set about each other in the good old nursery fashion, no quarter given. Looking back on it now, it seems to me that Lilibet was perhaps an unusually good child, though when she did rebel against authority she did it in her own particularly determined and final manner.

There came in those early days to 145 a certain Mademoiselle who taught French. Her methods consisted mainly in the writing out of endless columns of verbs. During these French lessons I used to play with Margaret in the drawing room next door.

One day curious sounds emerged from the schoolroom. I went in to see what had happened. I found poor Mademoiselle shattered and transfixed with horror. Lilibet, rebelling all of a sudden, and goaded by boredom to violent measures, had picked up the big ornamental silver inkpot and placed it without any warning upside down on her head. She sat there, with ink trickling down her face and slowly dyeing her golden curls blue. I never really got to the bottom of what had happened. Mademoiselle was past explaining, and had to retire and drink water while I coped with what Alah had to say.

Queen Mary had said to me, 'What a waste of time when you go away for holidays and the French lessons have to stop. They have the whole holidays and no language study at all. When I was a child I kept up my French and German, and had a certain amount of holiday work to do.'

So the Queen got Georgina Guérin, daughter of her former Mademoiselle, to come to the Princesses while I went on a holiday.

Margaret loved stories. She liked the same story over and over again, rather than a new one she did not know. She listened very intently and knew her favourites by heart. Her favourite was *The Little Red Hen*. She would stop me to correct me, 'Crawfie, you haven't said ...' It had to go exactly the same way every time.

But most of all they liked to look out of the windows in the evening, when the lights were lit in London streets, and the buses sailed by like galleons through the dusk. We would wait for our two friends, the brewer's horses, and watch them stand, steaming a little, on cold nights. The two little girls would hold their breath anxiously when the streets were slippery and it was not easy for the horses to get started again. From our perch up there we could see the lit windows of St George's Hospital at Hyde Park Corner, and the tangle of traffic coming down Park Lane. Then I would tell them another kind of story about the life that went on in the outside world, of which they knew so little, and of my home in Scotland, and the animals that I as a little girl had had as pets. They wanted to know all manner of things.

'Had you a little brother, Crawfie? How many bedrooms have you in your house? Have you got a garden? Did you have a hoop?'

Lilibet loved best the stories about real people, and it was in this way I presented history to her, as the doings not of a lot of dusty lay figures of the past, but of real people with all their problems and bothers. She would listen with rapt attention.

Lilibet was a very neat child. She kept her books and all her belongings immaculately tidy. But though no one ever tried harder or persevered more painstakingly, she never was any good with her needles. This I always felt was a disappointment to her grandmother, that indefatigable knitter, Queen Mary.

Presently I began to take the children about. We started quietly, leaving Hamilton Gardens one day by the private gate and walking out into the park. No one paid any attention to us, so we went farther afield. There was the Serpentine in Hyde Park, with its ducks and friendly birds and rowing-boats and sea-gulls to be visited, and we even got as far as the Round Pond near Kensington Palace on more than one occasion and watched other children sailing toy yachts.

Other children always had an enormous fascination, like mystic beings from a different world, and the little girls used to smile shyly at those they liked the look of. They would so have loved to speak to them and make friends, but this was never encouraged. I often have thought it a pity. The Dutch and Belgian royal children walked about the streets in their countries as a matter of course.

Only once were we beleaguered by the Press. A persuasive young man recognized the children and wanted to take a picture. I knew that if this happened it would be the end of our unofficial outings, so I drove him off mercilessly.

'Crawfie, you were savage,' Lilibet said, delighted. 'I am sure he thinks now that Crawfies bite!'

We explored Hyde Park and the gardens in this quite unofficial way. The little girls loved it. The Duke and Duchess apparently approved, for they made no comment whatever. Alah, I know, thoroughly disapproved, but I think even she was beginning to realize she could not keep her darlings safely cloistered for ever.

One day as we passed Hyde Park Corner people were streaming out of the underground station and Lilibet said wistfully, 'Oh, dear, what fun it must be to ride in those trains.' I thought, *why not?* It seemed such a simple request. I asked the Duke about it that evening.

As long as we had someone with us, neither of the children's parents objected in the least. So it was arranged that the house detective should accompany us at a discreet distance, and that the Duchess's lady-in-waiting, Lady Helen Graham, should also be one of this exciting party.

Anyone would have thought we were going on an expedition to the stately pleasure domes of Kubla Khan rather than for a ride in an underground train. The little girls bought their tickets out of their own purses. This was part of the fun. It always took them an immense time to get the money out and collect their change, and the whole business was solemn as an investiture.

Lilibet had a shilling a week pocket-money until she was

fourteen or fifteen. Mostly she just saved this up for the Christmas or summer holidays. Margaret did not get any pocket-money at all at this time. She never seemed to be very interested in it. Even when they were quite grown up the King would pass a shilling along to them in church, when the time came to put it in the plate. A pound note for himself and one for the Queen, and a shilling for each Princess. I provided my own. From time to time, Alah would generously present Margaret with a half-crown. This lasted her an immensely long time. They each had a little embroidered purse they kept in their handkerchief drawer.

The escalator to the underground seemed a perilous trip. Margaret's hand tightened on mine, and she swallowed apprehensively. Once safely on, down we sailed and caught our train. The little girls sat there very demurely, wide-eyed and enchanted, until suddenly at the far end of the same carriage we spotted our detective! He looked so very obviously a detective that people began to look round to try to discover what he was detecting. Mercifully, we arrived at Tottenham Court Road and got out before anyone had discovered the reason.

Our jaunt was to the YWCA. This had had to be planned ahead, but we still tried to keep it entirely unofficial, and few there knew who the children were. We collected our own tea on trays with the rest of the clientele. Lilibet left her teapot behind. The lady in charge bawled out to her, 'If you want it you must come and fetch it.' Tea out of thick cups, other people's bread and butter, tea you paid for with money, these were wonderful treats.

That afternoon our fun was rather spoiled because someone recognized them, word went round, and crowds began to gather. I sent a hasty message from the office for a car to be sent from the Duke's garage, and we had to drive home.

The next grand occasion was to be a ride on a bus. On *top*

of a bus. Lilibet insisted. It seemed to her such a wonderful idea that when you were on top of a bus you would be able to see right into other people's gardens. Sad to tell, these pleasant jaunts came to a sudden end. The Irish Republican Army started about this time to put bombs in letter-boxes, and to commit other public nuisances to draw attention to their demand for Home Rule for Ireland. It was not quite certain in what even less desirable directions their efforts might not lead them if it were known that the two Princesses were often afoot in London, unprotected.

We went back to our games of Indians and hide-and-seek and horse fairs in Hamilton Gardens.

CHAPTER III

The Close of the Reign

I was at 145 Piccadilly for four years. Lilibet was now ten. She was a long, slender, very beautifully-made child, with a mop of golden hair. No two children had a simpler outlook on life. Early bed and very few treats or outings, and those of an extremely unsophisticated nature, were the common rule. They never went to the seaside yearly as most other English children do. They had one pantomime a year. In those happy pre-war days, theatre managers always had a large box of chocolates in the royal box. But the little girls' great ambition was to sit in the stalls or the dress circle. They had to hang over the side of the royal box, to see properly. I can still see the Duke anxiously seizing his daughters' petticoats, afraid they would fall over altogether in their immense enthusiasm.

The children looked forward to these pantomimes for the remaining eleven months of the year. Margaret, as soon as she could talk at all, would re-enact most of the parts for her own edification in a corner of the nursery.

They always went to the horse show at Olympia with their parents, after which the toy horses round the dome would be put through several weeks of intensive training. They seldom had other children to tea. It was a quiet and homelike life, the children seeing a great deal more of their parents than most London society children do.

We learned to dance reels. Both the Duke and Duchess used to come in after lunch occasionally and join in. In winter we used to open all the communicating doors and play hide-and-seek over the whole house.

In those early years I saw very little of King George and Queen Mary. We always looked for their pictures in the newspapers, and Margaret used to lie on her tummy on the schoolroom floor and carefully pick them both out.

The Princess Royal (Aunt Mary, the Duke's sister) came now and again to tea, but not very often. She was an ultra-devoted mother and seldom left her two little boys. The Prince of Wales (Uncle David) was perhaps the most constant visitor. He was very fond of his brother, and he was devoted to Lilibet. He often took part in their after-tea games – snap, and happy families. He gave Lilibet all the A. A. Milne children's books – *Winnie the Pooh*, *When We Were Very Young*, and the others. Both little girls knew most of the poems by heart, and needless to say their favourite one was 'Changing the Guard at Buckingham Palace'.

The Duke and Duchess rarely dined out. In the evening, the happy bath hour over, the children bedded and the day's work done, they would sit one each side of the fireplace like any other young married couple, happy in each other, not requiring any outside diversion. The Duke was astonishingly expert with a needle. He once made a dozen chair covers in *petit point* for Royal Lodge. I remember he got rather tired of filling in the background, so I obliged with that while he went on with the more amusing part of the design.

Rarely was there a dinner party. They were happiest alone. As in those days they had fewer social obligations, they were able to do as they wished. They seldom went to a cinema or a theatre.

The high spot of the day remained the bedtime hour. The children had their tea at five, and contrary to the usual

English custom, which ends nursery meals there except for a glass of milk and some biscuits, had quite a substantial supper just before bedtime. They always ended up with an apple while they sat up in bed.

After tea they joined their parents. Endless games of rummy and racing demon went on till six or half past, when Alah called for Margaret. Racing demon is a card game that must be played very quickly. The cards are laid out on the table, and have to be snatched up, the one who gets all her cards first being the winner. This always entailed a good deal of scratching, rather in the way of honourable wounds received in battle.

When both children were in the bath, the Duke and Duchess would go upstairs to them. Hilarious sounds of splashing could be heard coming from the bathroom. Later, pillow fights in the bedroom would set Alah begging them not to get the children too excited. There was a weighing machine in the nursery, where weights and measures were ceremoniously noted down. Perhaps they still are, but from a different angle now.

Then, arm in arm, the young parents would go downstairs, heated and dishevelled and frequently rather damp, under the big dome with its circle of horses. The children called to them as they went, until the final door closed, 'Good night, Mummie. Good night, Papa!'

After dinner at eight-fifteen, the Duke and Duchess would mostly sit by the fire and talk, or read. I dined in my own room, free to go out if I chose, or to have a friend to dinner with me in the schoolroom. The Duke and Duchess went to bed about midnight. They were always called at eight in the morning.

Little did any of us dream then how one day not so far distant a bomb was to drop through that same glass dome and reduce the happy house to a heap of rubble. Where once it stood, there is now a gap in the row of houses on the terrace, like a missing tooth in a smile. Only the ground floor has been rebuilt.

It was, I believe, a worry to Queen Mary that the custom of family prayers, still upheld at the Palace, was not kept at 145 Piccadilly. The Duke and Duchess had allowed this sometimes uncomfortable ceremony to lapse. But there was something about that house that was in the best sense deeply religious, though perhaps not entirely conventionally so. The Duchess read her children Bible stories, and taught them their collects and psalms as she herself had been taught them, in the old Scottish paraphrased version that we who come from north of the border find so much more beautiful because it is what we are accustomed to.

It was at Royal Lodge, Windsor, during one of our happy weekends, that I discovered the children had considerable talent for acting. It started one day in the woods there when we played charades, just the three of us – one-man charades, in which each of us took it in turn to act someone we knew, and the others had to guess who it was.

There was never any doubt about Margaret's efforts! They were unmistakable. She kept us in fits of laughter with this first manifestation of a talent that was one day to amuse a much larger circle. The gift of fun-poking – and very clever fun-poking – Margaret had from an early age in a very large quantity.

Lilibet never had it to anything like the same extent. She was always a more serious child, though she, like her Aunt Mary, has a dry, humorous way of putting things.

Margaret's imagination led her along strange paths. Her dreams were appalling, and the telling of them was one of her ways of postponing the start of an unpopular lesson, or some chore she disliked. Just as in earlier days she had used the handy 'Cousin Halifax', it was now, 'Crawfie, I *must* tell you an amazing dream I had last night', and Lilibet would listen with me, enthralled, as the account of green horses, wild-elephant stampedes, talking cats, and other remarkable manifestations went into two or three instalments. Margaret was never at a loss. One of her early sayings achieved immortality.

When she was still a very small child, J. M. Barrie came over to tea at Glamis, from Kirriemuir, which he had made immortal under the name of Thrums. While they were at tea, there was a cracker lying on a plate between them, and he asked the little girl, jokingly, whether it belonged to her or to him.

Margaret said gracefully, 'It is yours *and* mine.'

J. M. Barrie put that line into his play *The Boy David*, and he gave Margaret one penny for every time it was used on the stage. The tale soon got about, and did a great deal to disperse the story of Margaret's being deaf and dumb.

After Barrie died, Lady Cynthia Asquith, who had been his secretary for many years, came to Buckingham Palace and brought Margaret all the pennies owed to her, in a bag.

Christmas was always looked forward to and prepared for months ahead. The Duchess would take the children shopping at Harrods. The children made their shopping lists up well ahead. The bulk of their purchases, however, came from Woolworth's. We went round the store ourselves and bought china ornaments, sweets, and pages of coloured stick-on scraps and transfers.

They were unsophisticated about presents, and the smallest gift gave an immense amount of pleasure. After they outgrew toy horses, books made up the great part of their gifts from Queen Mary and their uncles and aunts. Queen Mary gave them all the classics – Robert Louis Stevenson, Jane Austen, and Kipling. Others weighed in with book tokens.

The Duke and Duchess gave them small silver bracelets such as all little girls love. One year when they had been loaded with chocolates and all kinds of expensive presents, what pleased both of them more than anything else were small ladybird brooches given to them by Lilibet's nursemaid, Bobo.

Lilibet used to help Margaret laboriously with her shopping and presents lists, and I found among my papers the other day one of these, written in Lilibet's hand, to help Margaret write her thank-you letters, and remind her what she had received, and from whom it came. I give the list just as she wrote it.

Present	*Given*
See Saw	Mummie
Doll with dresses	"
Umbrella	Papa
Teniquoit	"
Brooch	Mummie
Calendar	Grannie
Silver Coffee Pot	Lilibet
Clock	to
Puzzle	Margaret
Pen and Pencil	Equerry
China field mice	M.E.
Bag and Cricket set	Boforts
Electric Stove	David B.L.
China lamb	Linda

There was always a great deal of consultation as to what should be given to Alah and Bobo. The latter, I seem to remember, came in for a lot of rather highly-coloured bath salts in her day!

Making up the Christmas parcels was great fun, and much skilful manoeuvring always went on, so that I should by no means guess what it was they had got for me. Once they gave me a small box for my mother. Inside was an elephant of ivory on a pin. On the back of the box was written the price. I have it to this day. Another year the two children gave me a bead necklace made like bunches of grapes.

I wish I had kept some of their letters written to Santa Claus. They were long and confiding, and the requests under the circumstances were most unambitious ones. Horses featured largely. Lilibet always got hold of Christmas catalogues and marked all the horsy books.

When Christmas came they duly hung out their stockings. And Papa and Mummie crept up, when at last the children slept, to fill them. They always had, besides this, one of those made-up net stockings full of pleasant little rubbishes – comic books, whistles, little balls, small tin frying-pans, and other nonsenses. They loved these dearly and kept all the empty ones year after year carefully put away.

There came a time much later on when they were all taken out and refilled for children in hospitals. Nothing was ever wasted. Lilibet had a large box into which she put every piece of ribbon off chocolate boxes and bouquets, neatly folded up, to be used again, and she kept every piece of silk or pretty coloured paper that took her fancy.

Another thing they loved to do at Christmas-time was to go down to the kitchens to help the cook, Mrs MacDonald (whom they called Golly, perhaps because she did look a bit like a golliwog), to stir the Christmas puddings. Golly made wonderful cakes for the blind soldiers, and we all used to help decorate them with silver horseshoes and bells, and those

bright silver pills dear to confectioners. Golly had great boxes
full of these things, and of coloured jellied sweets, in those old
spacious days. A good bit of tasting was enjoyed by all.

They were never greedy children. Their favourite sweet
was a certain fudge that Bobo, the nursery maid who is now
Lilibet's personal maid, used to make for them in the kitchen
from her own secret recipe which she guarded jealously. They
were apt to hoard that and be a little uneager to hand it round.
In general, a complete absence of any kind of lavishness was
the family rule.

On Queen Mary's birthday the children took her little
Victorian posies. All the birthday presents would be laid out
on Her Majesty's tables in her apartments. When we had all
made our curtsies and she had kissed us, she would tell us we
might each choose from among them something for ourselves.
Lilibet would scan the collection to see if there was anything
there to do with a horse; and if not, choose some other small
china animal, or little china dish. The presents the family gave
and received were all very simple, with a personal touch. One
felt the donors had always erred, if at all, on the side of
economy.

Queen Mary through all the years was an immense help and
comfort to me personally.

I sent Lilibet's school schedule at the time to Queen Mary
and received, in return, a number of helpful suggestions from
Her Majesty.

Lady Cynthia Colville replied on her behalf. She said that
Queen Mary was intensely interested in the timetable and had
commanded her to thank me very much for sending it. It had
struck Her Majesty as being a wonderfully ingenious curricu-
lum, considering how many subjects had to be included, and
in view of the fact that the afternoons were devoted to dancing, music, exercise, etc. There were a few questions that had

occurred to the Queen and she would very much like to know what I thought about them.

As regards History – two and a half hours a week seemed very little for this subject, but perhaps that couldn't be helped. But, for instance, was Arithmetic really more valuable – anyhow to them – than History? These two would probably never have to do even their own household books – but History? Princess Elizabeth's future career? Would it be worth while robbing a period or so of Arithmetic to add to History?

Of course, old-fashioned Geography was hopelessly out of date. But for them, all the same, a rather detailed knowledge of physical geography might be valuable, and also of the Dominions and India.

Her Majesty felt that I had allotted too little time to Bible reading.

Poetry. Did they ever learn poetry by heart? Rather an old-fashioned practice, too, and often overdone. But was not a little of it rather wonderful memory-training, and would it not help to 'get through' a good deal of first-rate interesting stuff which otherwise they might never read?

Her Majesty felt that genealogies, historical and dynastic, were very interesting to children, and, for these children, really important.

Did they learn script-writing? Her Majesty thought they wrote very well, but she had a great dislike for 'script'.

Lady Cynthia added that Queen Mary was anxious that I should receive these criticisms and comments in the kindly manner in which they were intended – she was thrilled about their education and, like me, wanted them to be absolutely perfect!

Queen Mary's practical suggestions were most welcome, of course, and I revised the schoolroom schedule for Princess Elizabeth accordingly:

MONDAY	TUESDAY	WEDNESDAY	THURSDAY	FRIDAY	SATURDAY
9.30 Bible	Arithmetic	Arithmetic	Arithmetic	Arithmetic	9.30–11.00 Résumé of week's work General Reading
10.00 History	Grammar	Geography	History	Writing and Composition	
10.30 Grammar	History	Literature	Poetry	History	
11.00 to 12.00 Break for elevenses (orange juice) and games in Hamilton Gardens					11.00–12.20 Riding
12.00 to 1.00 A rest: One half-hour for silent reading and one half-hour when I read to Princess Elizabeth. This covered a good deal of literature.					
1.15 Lunch					1.15 Lunch
Dancing Class or an educational visit with Queen Mary	Singing Class at Lady Cavan's house More walks or out to tea	Drawing Lesson	Music Lesson	Left for Royal Lodge every Friday afternoon	Out in garden and park with Duke and Duchess

Later it became extremely difficult to work to any definite plan. Lilibet was always being called away by Mummie or Papa. I had to adapt the work then and make use of any spare moments I had. Ours was never the entirely conventional schoolroom, and from my point of view the period at Birkhall and the five years I had the children alone at Windsor were a godsend as far as the work was concerned. We were uninterrupted.

During the morning break we used to go out and play in Hamilton Gardens, and the Duke often joined us. One of the favourite games and one at which he excelled was hopscotch, played on a roughly-marked-out court which can be either chalked on stones or scratched with a stick on the ground. It is played with a nice flat stone, and the idea is to kick the stone from square to square, hopping meantime. Both your feet on the ground, and you are out.

The Duke played with great precision of footwork, his daughters watching him critically.

Lilibet never objected to her daily period of lying down as long as it did not exceed half an hour. After that she became restless. She was always allowed to read a book at this time. Though both children went to bed early, they did not always remain there. There was a good bit of romping about.

The children's taste in books was a wide one. Though for a long time the *Black Beauty* type of story held first place with both of them, they loved all the Dr Doolittle stories, by Hugh Lofting, and were, in common with children the world over, very sad when Mr Lofting laid down his pen and firmly announced there would be no more. They liked *Lamb's Tales from Shakespeare*, but strangely enough never cared for *Alice in Wonderland*. They thought it rather stupid. I often wondered whether, had a horse played a leading part in it instead of a White Rabbit, their verdict might have been different. Thackeray's *The Rose and The Ring*, a mature work for young children, they liked very much indeed. When they were out of humour with me, I was often called Gruffenough, after the governess in the story.

Margaret had one treasured work that was all her own. It was a thumbed and torn penny dreadful, a tale of blood and pirates she found one day in an old box at Glamis Castle. She uncurled and flattened its yellow pages, and took great pains to repair it. For a time it was her favourite reading. She was very secretive about it and would not let anyone else see it.

I had always borne in mind King George's instructions to me about the Princesses' handwriting, and had avoided the sloping script he so objected to. Lilibet wrote a good clear hand entirely characteristic, and later on so did Margaret. They were both good letter writers, and I always heard very regularly from them during the holidays.

Music lessons were started early. Miss Mabel Lander began to come regularly to 145 Piccadilly. Lilibet was naturally musical and loved her lessons, but she hated to practise. Miss Lander was to find that Lilibet's wonderful memory and good ear were great drawbacks, and kept her from learning to read. She so soon got a tune off by heart, and could pick out on the piano by herself the songs the barrel-organs played and the butchers' boys whistled. Margaret started music lessons at seven and had a real gift, no doubt inherited from her other grandmother, Lady Strathmore, who had great talent.

We went to a singing class in the Countess of Cavan's home in Princes Gate for some time, and the children loved it. It came to an end when we moved to Buckingham Palace, but I formed a Madrigal Society at Windsor during the war, and that continued at the Palace until a year ago.

Both children had delightful speaking and singing voices from the earliest age. Margaret could sing all the *Merry Widow* tunes long before she could talk. They both picked up tunes with amazing ease, and it was charming to hear them sing duets together. This was something that always gave the Duke a lot of pleasure and amazement. He had always found it so difficult to do anything in public. To his little girls it came with the greatest ease.

Margaret, had she been trained, would undoubtedly have become a very good singer. As it is, her undoubted talent has given immense pleasure to her parents' visitors in the family circle. She is a born comic into the bargain, and accompanies herself for these turns on the piano in an almost professional manner.

Wireless was in its infancy then, and the children took little interest in it. But later both were *Itma* fans, and great admirers of Tommy Handley. Dinner was always a little earlier on the *Itma* nights so that they would not miss any of it. They also liked *Much-Binding-in-the-Marsh*. The King and Queen are great radio fans.

King George V was devoted to his grandchildren. He seemed to me to be especially fond of Lilibet. His own children had always been a little afraid of him, with his Victorian discipline, his quarter-deck voice, and his general strictness. Lilibet had none of these qualms. She was even at times a trifle patronizing. I remember on one occasion when he drew a rather unhandy picture for her, she stood at his elbow, watching, encouraging him.

'You really are not at all a bad drawer,' she told him kindly.

It was wonderful to see them together, the bearded old man and the polite little girl holding on to one of his fingers. When he was so ill, a part of the tonic his doctors recommended for his convalescence was her presence. She was then four years old. She went down with him to Bognor Regis. It was the first time she had ever been to the sea. She used to play about on the sand while the old King sat in the sunshine, watching her.

We were supposed to go and play in the Palace gardens whenever we cared to, but for some reason this was never a popular expedition and smacked too much of putting on good clothes and having to behave. The children infinitely preferred the small smutty enclosure of Hamilton Gardens. Perhaps just because it meant home.

At this time the whole family went up to Birkhall for the summer holidays. This is a small Stuart house built in 1715 on the banks of the River Muick, just outside Ballater in Scotland. It is Victorian inside, with pine-wood furniture and masses of Landseers. Landseer had been Queen Victoria's drawing master in her childhood, and she was a great admirer of all his works. The staircases are lined with Spy's caricatures. Some of these caricatures have personal letters attached to the backs of them, and we spent many wet days reading them. There was hardly a great statesman from Victoria's time up to the present day not represented there, and these I found a great help with history.

Birkhall is whitewashed outside and has a dark pine porch at the front door. Queen Victoria had these porches put on all the royal houses so that she could get into her carriage without getting blown to pieces on windy days.

The bedrooms are very simple and Victorian, with pinewood beds and old-fashioned washstands with the customary chinaware. In the King's bathroom there is one text: CLEANLINESS IS NEXT TO GODLINESS.

As in Buckingham Palace and Windsor Castle, there are three basins in a line, each with hot and cold water. One marked for 'teeth', one 'hands', and one 'face'!

When I first went to Birkhall it was lit by oil lamps, and very smelly oil stoves were carried up to the bedrooms in bitter weather. Since then it has been brought up to date.

Just as her father and mother did before her, Princess Elizabeth now has Birkhall as her summer residence. It has been given her. Her children will play in the same nurseries she shared with her sister.

It had been obvious for some time that the old King's health was failing. He had made a wonderful recovery from his serious illness, but he had never been quite the same person again. There was suddenly a vagueness about him. His booming voice had quietened; he was in every way more gentle.

Nothing seemed particularly imminent, however, when I went up to Scotland for my usual Christmas holiday. The first I personally knew of how serious matters had suddenly become was when the message was broadcast to the nation and we knew the end was near: 'The King's life is moving peacefully to its close.'

I had a telegram almost immediately asking me to return to Royal Lodge, Windsor, where the children were. I had had a tooth out the day before. Cocaine never goes through my face; it sat there like an apple on my cheek, and I looked as though I had been crying my eyes out. I can still remember the sort of hush that had fallen over England. All the way down south the stations were strangely silent and empty, and everyone looked sad. People had not realized how much they loved the old King until he was dead.

At Royal Lodge two little figures were waiting for me. The Duke and Duchess had gone to town and left a message for me: 'Don't let all this depress them more than is absolutely necessary, Crawfie. They are so young.'

I kept them in Windsor until all arrangements had been made for the funeral, then I took them to London. Margaret was much too young to pay attention to what was going on. She was intrigued by the fact that Alah from time to time burst into a flood of tears.

Lilibet in her sensitive fashion felt it all deeply. It was very touching to see how hard she tried to do what she felt was expected of her. I remember her pausing doubtfully as she groomed one of the toy horses and looking up at me for a moment.

'Oh, Crawfie ... ought we to play?' she asked.

I said certainly they ought to play, and that the last thing anyone you loved would wish you to do was to sit round and be miserable. But it was not very easy to keep them cheerful in that suddenly muted house. We played, I remember, endless games of noughts and crosses – a game I can't contemplate to this day without hearing in my ears the strains of the Dead March from *Saul*.

We fuss needlessly about the young. I remember I was very bothered at the thought of Lilibet going to the lying-in-state. She was so young, I thought. What could she possibly know of death? But she had to go. She drove off with the Duke and Duchess, in her black coat and black velvet tammy, looking small and, I thought, rather scared. The streets were filled with the usual great crowds, but now they were all silent.

All Lilibet saw as they filed past the raised dais were great heaps of flowers. At this time the King's sons stood on guard. How relieved I was to find that what had impressed itself on Lilibet was how still they stood.

'Uncle David was there,' she told me, 'and he never moved at all, Crawfie. Not even an eyelid. It was wonderful. And everyone was so quiet. As if the King were asleep.'

Margaret bounced around, happily unconscious of everything, in her nursery on the day of the funeral, but Lilibet had to go. The whole long ceremony would have been too much for her, we decided, so it was arranged that I should take her to Paddington Station quietly in time to see the gun-carriage with the King's body coming down the ramp. The Duke wanted her to see that, and to have that memory.

So, with the small, forlorn-looking figure in its inky black, off I went. The procession, as is common to processions, had taken longer than anyone expected. We arrived at Paddington Station an hour and a half too soon. It was difficult to know how to pass the time. The place was packed with silent and often weeping people. It was a depressing business in the naturally gloomy and vaulted station for a little girl to endure.

A kindly stationmaster put us into his private room, where we once again played endless games of noughts and crosses on Great Western Railway note paper. From time to time I felt anxious about Lilibet, for she was very white. But children have a way of taking these trying events in their stride.

When we heard the bands playing and saw the gun-carriage covered with the Union Jack come slowly into sight, for a moment she realized what it all meant and her small face quivered. But a wonderful diversion occurred at exactly the right moment. One of the sailors marching there fainted just below us. The ranks on either side of him immediately closed in on him, holding him up and marching him along with the rest. Lilibet was so enchanted with the cleverness of this pro-ceeding that the sad moment passed. I wished the young sailor who fainted could have known what a diversion he caused for a little girl on a sad day.

I had to take Lilibet down on to the platform where she was to join her father and mother on the Windsor train. Here I struck a snag we had not thought of. All the royal ladies were draped from head to foot in black crepe, their faces covered. I stood for a moment lost and bewildered, very conscious of my uncovered face and not quite certain what to do next.

The Duchess realized my difficulty. She raised one hand and beckoned to us. Lilibet ran over and stood there, holding on to her with that look on her small face I knew so well. She did not much like all this, but she meant to go through with it, making no fuss.

After the funeral, life settled down quickly for the children, who, happily, soon forget.

Let it not be thought that all was sweetness and light in our schoolroom all the time. These were two entirely normal and healthy little girls, and we had our difficulties. Neither was above taking a whack at her adversary, if roused, and Lilibet was quick with her left hook! Margaret was more of a close-in fighter, known to bite on occasions. More than once have I been shown a hand bearing the royal teeth marks. They scrapped over their toys in an entirely healthy manner from

time to time. Schoolroom brawls often started when they had
to wear hats. They hated hats. This put them in a bad humour,
and they would snap one another's elastic to shrill cries of
'You brute! You beast!' 'Margaret always wants what I want,'
was the common complaint. Perhaps the Duchess thought
this boded no good for the future.

Of the two children, Lilibet was the one with the temper,
but it was under control. Margaret was often naughty, but she
had a gay bouncing way with her which was hard to deal with.
She would often defy me with a sidelong look, make a scene
and kiss and be friends and all forgiven and forgotten. Lilibet
took longer to recover, but she had always the more dignity of
the two.

The Duke was immensely proud of her. He had a way of
looking at her that was touching. But Margaret brought
delight into his life. She was a plaything. She was warm and
demonstrative, made to be cuddled and played with. At one
time he would be almost embarrassed, yet at the same time
most touched and pleased, when she wound her arms round
his neck, nestled against him and cuddled and caressed him.
He was not a demonstrative man.

Lilibet took after him. She, too, was reserved and quiet
about her feelings. If you once gained her love and affection
you had it for ever, but she never gave it easily. Only once did
she walk right into my arms, thinking of nothing but that for
the moment she had to have a little comforting. That was
when she came into my room, very white and wide-eyed.

'Oh, Crawfie, Grandfather Strathmore is dead,' she said,
and burst into tears.

Lord Strathmore, the Duchess's father, was a most gentle and
humorous person. He was a countryman through and
through. He timed all his movements by country things – the
coming of the migrants, the wild geese on the river, the rising

of the sap. This gave a particular atmosphere to Glamis itself, so that you felt you were much nearer to reality and nature there than at any other place.

He always made his cocoa for his breakfast himself, ate plum pudding for lunch every day of his life, and always had beside him at meals a small jug of water with which he diluted his wine. The little girls adored him, and he them, but they confided to me that his whiskers tickled.

He had a flowing silky moustache which he divided carefully in the centre before kissing them. Until he was very old indeed, he used to ride his pony into the woods and cut and tidy the trees. One of the keepers went with him. Sometimes on our walks we would come across the two of them, talking together as friends.

Glamis Castle stands in its own large grounds on the east coast of Scotland, between Edinburgh and Aberdeen. Sir John Lyon, founder of the family, who was Keeper of the Privy Seal to the King of Scotland in 1371, was granted what was then called the thanage of Glamis the following year. Like Windsor Castle, Glamis Castle started life as a fortress. It dates from 1033. Here dwelt Macbeth, who is reputed to be by no means the entirely vicious character Shakespeare makes him out to be in his play.

The real Macbeth, though said to have murdered Duncan, was otherwise a good enough king, as kings went in those days. Far from meeting a speedy death, as in the play, his reign lasted for seventeen years, and he gained the respect of his people. But there are tales enough, apart from that one, about the Castle. Malcolm II was killed there, and the Old Pretender stayed there in 1716. A Grey Lady is said to walk at night. And somewhere tucked away there is a small gloomy apartment called the Hangman's Room, where that worthy was put up when, as was the custom in those days, he did his rounds. Much as a judge when on circuit. There is the famous legend of the Glamis Monster. In some secluded tower they say it lurks, its horrid presence revealed to each heir on his attaining his majority. At night the old Castle is certainly full of odd rattles, and wailing winds, and strange noises. But I stayed there many times, and can only say I never witnessed any of these hauntings.

There was a wonderful atmosphere there, that seemed to belong to other and more peaceful days. Life revolved round the still-room and the big kitchens, where the children loved to go to taste the newly baked cakes and beg for coffee sugar.

From dusty boxes we would unearth old forgotten treasures, photographs, old manuscripts, and books. We would join the family for lovely peaceful teas in the Blue Room. The Countess of Strathmore was a wonderful personality. She was one of those people who make a happy atmosphere. The place had for the children the added charm that their mother had spent her childhood there. There were all the places to be visited Mummie had so often spoken of. There were all the stories to hear of 'when Mummie was a little girl'.

The children spent happy, carefree days there, full of simple but enchanting things to do. One of our favourite expeditions was to take the pony down to Glamis Station to watch the Aberdeen Fish Express go through. The pony was temperamental about trains, and the station master very kindly let us shut him up in the waiting-room. Unfortunately, one day when, as usual, we did this, the stationmaster had forgotten to warn us that he had put all his best chrysanthemums ready for the flower show in there. The pony ate the lot.

It was on Glamis railway station platform the little girls first discovered chewing-gum. A cousin who was staying there with them initiated them into its wonderful possibilities. Trains are few and far between there, and we had lots of time to place crossed pins stuck together with gum on the lines, and wait for the next train through to turn them into enchanting little scissors. The woods round Glamis were mostly gold and scarlet with autumn colours when we went there. There were wonderful crimson toadstools growing there, that looked as though they had been sugared over on top. We felt certain they must be deadly poison, until, one day sitting very quietly on a fallen tree there, we saw a large rabbit come out, and painstakingly nibble all round one of them, then polish his whiskers and amble happily away!

Those times at Glamis were really restful holidays for all of us. There were no eyes at the railings, there were no crowds except the birds. There were endless dressing-up chests full of old-fashioned frocks, and tapestries, and hats of other days, and pieces of silk, and room after room, and passage after passage, in which to play hide-and-seek and sardines. It was a fascinating place for children, and if the Thane of Glamis and the lurking monster left their shadows over it for some they never depressed us at all.

I don't know who was more sorry when the Glamis holidays came to an end, the children or I.

Both Lilibet and Margaret went through a tiresome time between the ages of six and twelve, when they bit their nails. What struggles I had with them over this. The business of curing them wasn't made any easier for me, either, when one day at some function the children attended we saw Mr Chamberlain himself with his fingers in his mouth, gnawing away. (His nanny, apparently, had had less success than I hoped to achieve.) Both Lilibet and Margaret nudged me in shocked and triumphant delight. Obviously, if the Prime Minister could do it, indulging to his heart's content in this furious sport, why not they?

They took great interest in the various prominent people who came and went, and passed some astonishingly acute judgements, too, on this one or that, from their perch on the top of the well under the dome at 145. Already Lilibet was developing a charming little manner of her own in company, and she made the most brave efforts to model herself on her mummie and always say the right thing at the right time. This was charming, but not always entirely successful. One day Ramsay MacDonald bent low over her small hand, and she said in that clear ringing voice of hers:

'I saw you in *Punch* this morning, Mr MacDonald, leading a flock of geese!'

Mr MacDonald gave her a wan smile.

CHAPTER IV

We Move to
Buckingham Palace

THE old reign had ended. Presently Queen Mary moved away from Buckingham Palace to Marlborough House. This is a big square house standing in its own beautiful garden behind a high brick wall, a stone's throw from the Palace. It is filled with beautiful things, including Queen Mary's collection of jade, of which she is very proud.

Of all the royal houses this is the most homelike and best kept, every floor and window always shining. Queen Mary's staff never want to leave her. Everyone who works for her loves her very much.

I remember at that time picking up a paper one night and seeing in the Court Circular an unfamiliar name. A Mrs Simpson was among the guests mentioned at the new King's country home, Fort Belvedere. I thought nothing of it at the time, but presently when the rumours and whispers that had long been going on in the world outside began to reach us, I remembered the name.

Though the foreign papers had long been full of gossip and strange speculations, it was not until the autumn of 1936 that the English papers brought themselves to mention her by name, except in the Court Circulars. All we at 145 Piccadilly knew in the schoolroom was that of a sudden we saw much less of handsome golden-headed Uncle David. There were fewer occasions when he dropped in for a romp with his nieces.

Then one day when we were all at Royal Lodge for the weekend he arrived to tea, bringing friends with him. Among them, Mrs Simpson. I looked at her with some interest. She was a smart, attractive woman, with that immediate friendliness American women have.

No one alluded to that visit when we met again later in the evening. As usual, nothing whatever was said, though I suppose most of us had the subject in our minds. Maybe the general hope was still that if nothing was said, the whole business would blow over.

But it was impossible not to notice the change in Uncle David. He had been so youthful and gay. Now he looked distraught, and seemed not to be listening to what was said to him. He made plans with the children, and then forgot them.

On 3 December 1936, the newspapers carried a grim headline: THE KING AND HIS MINISTERS. GREAT CONSTITUTIONAL CRISIS. I had been out. I bought an evening paper just outside in Hamilton Place, and I remember I read the headline while I waited for the front door to open.

Looking back, I can see now that it was really the end of a chapter. The peace of the house was broken. The cloud had appeared on the horizon. The uneasiness we all sensed in the air grew and did not diminish.

I do not know what we would have done at that time without the swimming lessons. They were a great diversion and took our minds off other matters.

The little girls were always very anxious to do whatever other children did. They longed to learn to swim, among other things, and I suggested this. The Duke and Duchess were wonderfully good about allowing these innovations, though some of the older members of the family, I feel, did not always approve.

The swimming lessons at the Bath Club did much to tide us over this anxious and difficult time, and to keep the children amused. We had, first of all, the fun of choosing bathing costumes and caps. This entailed a lot of trying on, with the Duke and Duchess watching. In the end they both had the Bath Club regulation dark blue swim suits, with initials in white, and white caps. Lilibet looked so pretty in hers. She was a long, slender child with beautiful legs. Margaret, everyone owned, looked like a plump navy-blue fish.

There was always a slight tension when the children went anywhere in this way. Public interest was great, and the Bath Club pool would often be crowded.

The swimming instructress at the Bath Club was Miss Amy Daly. She is to the young swimming world what Mrs Wordsworth, the famous London society dancing mistress, was to beginners in that other accomplishment. Miss Daly, when I went to see her and tell her she was to have the Princesses as pupils, was hot and bothered. What should she do? Should she curtsy? Ought the baths to be closed when the Princesses had their lessons? How should she treat the little girls?

I remember saying to her, 'After all, Miss Daly, everyone looks much the same in the water, you know! As far as you are concerned, they are meantime no different from Jane and Mary Smith. And they do so hate having any difference made.'

On our first trip Alah made preparations of such magnitude that we might all have been going out on a raft to a desert island. Large bath towels, dusting powder, combs and brushes, a small box of chocolates were all packed up into quite a large zip bag. I think had she had her way she would have added a couple of life-buoys. At first she was inclined to hover at the water's edge like a distressed hen that has mothered a couple of ducks. She was sure they would catch cold, or sink, or become frightened.

Miss Daly was wonderfully clever with Alah. After a time I think Alah realized this was a scene in which she did not appear, and she retired to the cubicle to guard her darlings' belongings, accompanied by her interminable knitting.

Alah incessantly knitted socks for a brother and nephew. Later when the war came her output of sea-boot stockings was stupendous. She was never seen without one gradually appearing off her diligent needles. How she struggled to teach Lilibet to knit! They started with long woollen garters for Papa's plus-four stockings. Lilibet was never much good with a needle of any kind, though no one tried harder. She simply had not got the knack. In many of her holiday letters to me the phrase occurs, accompanied I knew with a sigh, 'I am afraid I am not getting on very well with my needlework.'

The little girls were rather apprehensive on the first day, but something happened that did a lot to reassure them. When we went into the baths for the first time, a girl was standing poised on the highest step of the diving-board. Her arms out-stretched, her body straight, she was waiting.

Both the children's grip on my hands tightened, and Lilibet drew her breath with horror. Miss Daly said, 'Go', and we watched a most beautiful swan dive.

'I shall never be able to do that,' Lilibet said.

Miss Daly laughed. 'Oh, yes, you will. Probably far more easily than that girl – because she is blind. She has to trust me absolutely, whereas you can both see what you are doing.'

Miss Daly's method of teaching young children was an excellent one. She laid them over a wooden bench first and taught them the motions of swimming by asking them to make the letters Y, I, T, and X with their arms and legs. Lilibet was soon able to pick this up, but we had a lot of amusement out of Margaret, who was plump, and wobbled about on the bench.

'You look like an aeroplane about to conk out,' Lilibet laughed. 'Keep steady, Margaret!'

When the time came to get the children into the water I was glad the scheme to close the baths had not been carried out. It was a lot easier to get the little girls, especially Margaret, into the water when there were others in already. Just at the beginning Margaret showed a tendency to linger a long time on the top step, or cling to the side. Princess Elizabeth would call, 'Don't be a limpet, Margaret.' But when other children came along and just plunged in, she was soon doing the same.

The Duke and Duchess often came down to watch. It has always been an immense pleasure to the Duke to see his children accomplish things simply and easily, without any fuss, and in a way it never ceases to astonish him. 'I don't know how they do it,' he said to me more than once. 'We were always so terribly shy and self-conscious as children. These two don't seem to care.'

The children both ended by taking the Life Saving Certificate, which is quite an achievement in itself. This entailed plunging into the water fully dressed. Lilibet saved Margaret in fine style, and they were both given certificates which they were immensely proud of. Alas, they disappeared, among other treasures, during the blitz.

The outings to the swimming club were the high spots of the week during those rather uneasy times, and they helped a lot to take our minds off the clouds that were gathering about us all.

Perhaps it was the nervous tension of those days that affected me. I know I always felt slightly sick. I had a bad relaxed throat, among other things. One day Miss Longman, the singing mistress, was coming to tea. I said to Lilibet, 'I must go and gargle before she arrives. I feel as if my epiglottis had fallen down on my tongue.'

Miss Longman arrived a trifle early. Lilibet, doing the honours, received her graciously and said in her most grown-up manner, 'Crawfie will be back in a few minutes. Her epiglottis has just fallen out.'

Mine was an exceptionally difficult task. I had as far as possible to come between the children and the general upheaval and rumours, and carry on as though nothing out of the ordinary was happening.

I did what I could to keep the children happy during those uneasy days. We used to watch, down the well of the dome, important people coming and going. The Prime Minister, Mr Baldwin, bishops and archbishops passed below, all looking anxious and harried. The Duke and Duchess never spoke of what was happening, but it was plain to everyone there was a sudden shadow over the house. To make matters worse, the Duchess herself was far from well. In the end she went to bed with a bad cough and cold.

One afternoon the Duchess sent for me to go and see her. She was occupied when I reached her room, and I stood outside in an alcove by the landing window, waiting, and watching the crowds gathered below, who, like myself, were wondering what the next move was to be. And then something happened that told me that the abdication had taken place. The bedroom door opened. Queen Mary came out of the Duchess's room. She who was always so upright, so alert, looked suddenly old and tired.

The Duchess was lying in bed, propped up among pillows. She held her hand out to me.

'I'm afraid there are going to be great changes in our lives, Crawfie,' she said.

We talked for a little while as to how we were going to break this news to the children, and what differences it would make. The break was bound to be a painful one. We had all been so happy in our life at 145.

'We must take what is coming to us, and make the best of it,' the Duchess said with good sense.

When I broke the news to Margaret and Lilibet that they were going to live in Buckingham Palace they looked at me in horror.

'What!' Lilibet said. 'You mean for ever?' Margaret said, 'But I have only just learned to write "York".'

That weekend the whole family met at Royal Lodge for the farewell dinner. No servants were present. Only Ainslie the butler knows what passed then. It must all have been very harrowing and trying. I remember seeing the Duke's face for a moment as he came back late that night, no doubt with his elder brother's voice ringing in his ears with the words that ended that fateful broadcast: 'God Save the King!'

It was as the King and Queen that I had to think of them from that day on.

The proclamation took place on 12 December 1936. None of us from 145 went to hear it. The Queen was still in bed with her chill. It was left to me to make the two little girls realize that from this day onward great changes would take place.

Lilibet and Margaret had run as usual to give their father a final hug as he went off; looking very grave, dressed as an Admiral of the Fleet. I had to explain to them that when Papa came home to lunch at one o'clock he would be King of England, and they would have to curtsy to him. The royal children from their earliest years had always curtsied to their grandparents.

'And now you mean we must do it to Papa and Mummie?' Lilibet asked. 'Margaret too?'

'Margaret also,' I told her, 'and try not to topple over.'

When the King returned, both little girls swept him a beautiful curtsy. I think perhaps nothing that had occurred had brought the change in his condition to him as clearly as this did. He stood for a moment touched and taken aback. Then he stooped and kissed them both warmly. After this we had a hilarious lunch.

The King and the Queen went on ahead of us to the Palace. It was some little time before we joined them, though we used to go over and play in the gardens, and once we had tea with them in the magnificent Belgian Suite. These vast rooms are all done in pink-and-gold brocade, and have always to me resembled the setting of a luxurious pantomime. I sat down on a pink-and-gold chair. There was an ominous splitting sound, and it dissolved beneath me. It had not been recaned since Queen Victoria's day.

People think that a royal palace is the last word in up-to-date luxury, replete with everything the heart could desire, and that people who live there do so in absolute comfort. Nothing could be farther from the truth. Life in a palace rather resembles camping in a museum. These historic places are so old, so tied up with tradition, that they are mostly dropping to bits, all the equipment there decades behind the times.

Electric light had certainly been installed, but only quite recently; and the arrangements of this were often very odd. My bedroom light could be turned on and off only by a switch some two yards outside my doorway in the passage. The first night when the housemaid came to pull my bedroom curtains, the whole thing – curtains, pelmet, and heavy brass rods – came down with a clatter, narrowly missing our heads.

Though sad to leave 145 Piccadilly, the little girls, like children all the world over, were excited over the move. They spent a lot of time getting their fine stud of horses ready. The saddles all had to be strapped on, the grooming brushes and polishing cloths packed up into their big basket. I began to wonder if the little girls would want to wheel them all the way over to the Palace themselves, but in the end they went with other treasures in a furniture van. There they took up their stand in a long row down the corridor in the Palace outside the children's rooms. They were still there on Lilibet's wedding morning.

All this time there were incessant crowds outside the Palace, gazing up at it, obviously waiting for something to happen, though we could not imagine what. We in our turn used to gaze back at them through the lace curtains. It was a grand new amusement for the children on wet winter afternoons.

Their apartments faced the Mall. The little girls' nurseries had been repainted and done up, and were bright and cheerful. They each had a bedroom. Alah shared Margaret's room, while Bobo shared Lilibet's.

The question of a schoolroom was a problem. There was one. The King took me up to see it shortly after we were installed. It was one of the darkest and most gloomy rooms in the place, in the middle of the top floor of the Palace, facing the Mall. The heavy stone balustrade outside had the air of prison bars, and kept out the light. Enormous fireplaces, one at either end, had gloomy portraits hanging over them. The whole atmosphere was regal but oddly dead.

The King stood in the doorway for a few moments looking round in silence – no doubt remembering his own childhood spent up here, doing lessons on gloomy afternoons, the London fog yellow and thick outside the window, fingers stiff with the cold. And I thought how little he ever dreamed in those days of the circumstances in which he was to come back again.

I remember he turned away slowly, shutting the door behind him. 'No,' he said, 'that won't do.'

In the end we were given a small bright room looking out

over the gardens away from the Mall. It had been a nursery
for Lilibet when Queen Mary had looked after her while her
parents were abroad. It got the sun. The Victorians obviously
considered no one needed sun in their bedrooms. All faced
north. Only the big drawing rooms and State apartments
faced south over the gardens and the lake.

The Queen changed that in time, as she changed so much,
but I still recall with a shudder that first night spent in the
Palace. The wind moaned in the chimneys like a thousand
ghosts. I was homesick as I had not been for a long time, for
Scotland, and the simple life I had led there as a girl.

All this, I felt, was getting a bit out of hand. It was going to
be too much for me. At 145 Piccadilly it had been different.
We had been a small, utterly happy family. I did not think I
was going to like the change at all. Now we were separated
from one another by interminable corridors.

Buckingham Palace assumed its present form under
George IV in 1825. It was used as a London residence by
Queen Victoria. Edward VII was born, and died, there.
George V made extensive alterations to the place, and in his
reign for the first time it was really used as an official residence. The present King added the swimming pool, which
was unfortunately bombed. It got a direct hit.

The Palace now has heating in all the corridors, and there
are coal fires in bedrooms. It is soon going to be made entirely
up-to-date with a new oil-burning system, but that work is
proceeding slowly, as all work does in England today, and has
already been three years in hand.

We felt it was all far too big. It was five minutes' walk to
get out into the gardens. Whichever way you went, there were
those interminable corridors. Later I discovered the Vermin
Man who fought an endless battle against the mice. He had
some odd weapons. One he called a sticky trap. He offered to
put one in my bedroom, but I preferred the more conventional

kind. The sticky trap consists of a piece of cardboard with a lump of aniseed in the middle. This is surrounded by a sea of treacle with a dry inch all round to give the victim a footing. The mouse smells the aniseed and, trying to get at it, sticks to the treacle. I thought it a cumbersome method, but the Vermin Man thought highly of it, and he should know.

On my first morning at the Palace, when I crossed the corridor on the way to my bathroom, it was a shock to run into a postman. The Palace has its own post office, and letters are delivered to the various rooms. Just at first it was disconcerting, like walking in your dressing-gown into the main street.

It sounded strange to hear the little girls' happy voices, laughing and shouting as usual as they ran downstairs and along the corridors to Mummie's and Papa's room. In a very short time they set some of the ghosts to flight. The whole atmosphere changed and lightened. Many people there noticed this. 'It was as though the place had been dead for years, and had suddenly come alive,' they told me.

There was very little restraint placed on the children. The Prime Minister, coming to see the King on affairs of State, must have noticed the change. He might easily find himself tangled up with two excited little girls racing down the corridors. Or one stoutish little girl panting, 'Wait for me, Lilibet. Wait for me!' Perhaps Dookie, the Queen's devoted corgi, might take a nip at a passing leg. Dookie adored the taste of strange trousers.

It took us quite a while to settle down and get the old routine going again. I think we all of us rather felt we were camping in a desert. The house in Piccadilly had been so comfortable and quite small. Visitors had been mostly personal friends, and even they had been few and far between. The Palace was always full of people coming and going. With its post office, secretaries, privy purse, and all the rest of it, it was more like a village than a home.

The King and Queen must have thought often, regretfully, of their quiet evenings, one either side of the fire. They who had wanted only a simple life with their children were now besieged by photographers, pursued by Press agents, and harried by officials.

The King spent the morning in his study where he would be visited by his secretaries, then by the various ministers and ambassadors who had occasion to come. At one-fifteen the two little girls lunched with their parents if they were at home. I myself lunched with the household – the lady-in-waiting, the King's equerry, the Keeper of the Privy Purse, and other officials.

In the afternoon there would be some sort of function, or more visitors and documents claiming the King's attention. There would be a break for tea, after which the Prime Minister or one of the Cabinet ministers might come.

In the evenings there was always something doing. Their Majesties would have to attend a reception, a command performance, or a first night.

The Queen had her dressmakers. Between eleven and twelve she went through her letters with her lady-in-waiting and made up her engagement book. There was always a little queue of people waiting to see the Queen.

From twelve to one she would meet the ambassadors' wives. Occasionally I would meet the Queen in the middle of the morning in full evening dress, wearing her tiara. She would be sitting for one of the various painters who were doing her portrait.

In the afternoon the Queen had always a function of some sort. She never took the customary afternoon rest or nap. Often after the function was over she would come out and join us in the gardens, glad of a breath of fresh air. She would be enthusiastically welcomed by the dogs.

But no matter how busy the day was to be, the morning

sessions with the children began it. The children came first. Only the happy high jinks of the evening bath hour had to be curtailed and often abandoned. There was no longer time. Ahead, like a veritable Becher's Brook in the course of our lives, lay the Coronation. To a shy man, and one who had never courted any kind of publicity, the very thought must have been a nightmare.

I remember seeing the new King sitting solemnly at his desk one afternoon, painstakingly practising his new signature with a peculiarly sad expression on his face we had not seen previously. He had always signed himself 'Albert'. Now all of a sudden he was George R.I., and he had to practise it.

The best part of the Palace, as far as we were concerned, was the garden. There was a big lake in the middle which we found enchanting. Margaret asked me if the Mediterranean, which she had just met in geography, was as big as that. All kinds of amusing birds came there, and it had its own population of ducks. One of them, for reasons best known to herself, always laid her eggs and hatched them out in the smaller lake outside the Palace grounds. She then ceremoniously walked her children back to the Palace, over the courtyard and into the gardens. The police on duty stopped the traffic for her and opened the gates. The children were very interested in the private life of the ducks. One day I heard a splash and a shriek. I hastened to see what had happened, and saw Lilibet, covered with green slime, rising out of the water.

'Oh, Crawfie, I fell in,' she said, 'looking for the ducks' nest!'

We managed to smuggle her in and get most of the slime off her before Alah got news of it.

There was the summer house which King George had used during his last illness. It was just as he had left it, with his writing-table, pencils, and inkpot still there. This we adopted as an out-of-doors schoolroom.

Another very favourite place was a hill at the end of the garden. From there we could look out into the wide world. The automobiles went tearing down Buckingham Palace Road, and we could see the people passing, and other children with their nurses, bound for the park. These children were a source of interest, and Margaret was always enchanted by their clothes.

One day I remember a little boy went by riding a bicycle. 'One day,' said the heir to the throne dreamily, 'I shall have a bicycle.'

We could hear scraps of people's conversation floating up to us there. One day we saw the Queen go by in a car.

'It's Mummie,' shrieked Margaret delightedly, waving wildly though the car was out of sight.

Lilibet was very motherly with her younger sister. I used to think at one time she gave in to her rather more than was good for Margaret. Sometimes she would say to me, in her funny responsible manner, 'I really don't know what we are going to do with Margaret, Crawfie,' and go on to tell me of something she had been up to.

Margaret soon joined us at lessons. It was not a very easy matter to teach, at the same time, two children of such different ages, character, and development. The advent of a born comic never makes for peace in any schoolroom. Margaret had a way, when she knew I was cross with her, of fixing me with those beautiful blue eyes of hers, and saying persuasively, 'Crawfie! Laugh!' So often, alas, I had to laugh.

Bedtimes of necessity became movable, with the little girls waiting in hopes of seeing Mummie and Papa dressed for this function or that before they went off, or lying awake later than they should have done in the hopes of a good-night visit and kiss.

This bothered Alah and me a lot, but it seemed useless trying to make any changes until after the Coronation. The little girls' lives were all upset anyhow. They were always being taken from lessons to try on clothes or to have a look at something their parents felt they ought not to miss.

We all found the distances in Buckingham Palace wearing. It was a day's march to get from one end of it to the other. The food had to come from the kitchens to the dining rooms all the way from the Buckingham Palace Road end to the Constitution Hill end. The better part of half a mile, along corridors, and up and down stone steps. One day when we were exploring, Lilibet said dryly, 'People here need bicycles.'

The State apartments are all on the ground floor, overlooking the gardens. They are used only for banquets. When the family are by themselves, they dine in a simple little dining room on the second floor, close to their own apartments. Horse pictures, mostly I believe by Munnings, cover the walls. A square polished table, a sideboard, some chairs, and a screen furnish it. On the table there is always a pad and pencil, to put down notes. The colouring there is soft and pretty, the carpet the Queen's favourite beige.

The children had their supper in the nursery. The nursery footman brought up the dishes and put them on a hot-plate there. In the nursery they kept to the old-fashioned white tablecloth. Each child kept her table napkin neatly folded in a silver ring with her name on it. There was always something very pleasant and intimate about these nursery meals.

Mice continued to be a menace. One day when I went to my bath I found a large one sitting on my towel. The passing postman came in handy. Quaking, I gave him my poker and asked him to kill it. He put his bag of letters down and kindly obliged.

The Coronation, so long prepared for, was now upon us. Margaret was just a child, not yet seven years old. Lilibet was eleven. I was bothered as to how Margaret would come through the long, tiring ceremonies. She was so very young. When the day arrived, the children were up very early and down, as usual, to see their parents. There was a great deal of squealing and laughing and peeping out of the windows at the crowds that had already gathered the previous night. There is little sleep for anyone in the Palace on these occasions. The noise and the shouting and the singing go on all night long.

The King had taken immense interest in the children's outfits. We had had one scene when Margaret found Lilibet was to wear a little train, while she had none! They both wore lace frocks with little silver bows, and cloaks edged with ermine. The King had special coronets made for them, very light. I did not see the children that morning until they were dressed. They came to me very shyly, a little overawed by their own splendour and their first long dresses.

'Do you like my slippers?' Lilibet said, lifting her skirt to show me her silver sandals. I also saw that she was wearing short socks that revealed a length of honest scratched brown leg! Then we all went together to see the King and Queen in their robes. I remember thinking the little Queen looked most regal in all the jewellery and splendour. It was a great contrast with those other days, when she used to wear tweeds on the moors.

Cousins and aunts arrived, and the pages came. They are the sons of peers, appointed at the King's discretion. His Majesty pays them a goodly sum per year which in former times was intended as a tactful way of paying for the pages' education. To be a page is an honour greatly sought after. These pages are most beautifully dressed. The duties are mostly traditional.

On this occasion, among the pages chosen to bear the King's train were Earl Haig, Earl Jellicoe, Lord Herschell, Earl Kitchener, George Hardinge, son of the King's private secretary, and Alexander Ramsay, son of Rear-Admiral Sir A.R.M. Ramsay and Princess Pat.

I was extremely glad the long, slow drive to the Abbey was being made by carriage and not by car. Royal cars are always hermetically sealed and very stuffy. Their occupants must arrive without a hair out of place, so to open any windows is out of the question. How often have I watched, with anxiety, the little girls growing paler and paler, and I myself have frequently had to get out and walk the last part of the journey lest worse befall!

There was always something exciting in going in one of the big horse-drawn carriages. Lilibet and Margaret drove to the Abbey with Queen Mary. Margaret was so small that her place in the carriage had a specially built-up seat, to allow a little girl to see out of the window and wave to the crowds, which she did with much enthusiasm.

Lilibet was perturbed on Margaret's account. 'I do hope she won't disgrace us all by falling asleep in the middle, Crawfie,' she said anxiously. 'After all, she is *very* young for a coronation, isn't she?'

For the Coronation ceremony the various canons' rooms were converted to dressing rooms for the Royal Family. Dressing-tables and long mirrors were added.

Alah took the Princesses' brushes and combs. The King had his own separate robing room with his own valet in attendance. His Groom of the Robes, Sir Harold Campbell, was also in attendance. This is an honorary appointment and carries with it responsibility for seeing that the King has all the right garments and insignia put on in the right way. Quite a complicated business at a coronation. The Queen has the Mistress of the Robes to perform the same function for her, but this does not carry nearly so much responsibility.

There was a cold buffet arranged in one of the side rooms, with sandwiches and coffee, for a coronation is a lengthy proceeding. We left the Palace before eleven in the morning, and it was five in the afternoon before the whole show was finished – a lengthy day for little girls aged six and eleven.

When they finally got home again I asked Lilibet, 'Well, did Margaret behave nicely?'

'She was wonderful, Crawfie. I only had to nudge her once or twice when she played with the prayer books too loudly.'

They were all tired after the long service, but their duties were not yet over. Besides all the balcony appearances that are always called for again and again, there came the photographers. The little girls had to stand about having their pictures taken for the best part of an hour.

'We aren't supposed to be human,' the Queen once said, rather sadly.

Now the best part of all our lives were the weekends when we escaped from the Palace and all its glories and went down to Royal Lodge, Windsor. It is a mile and a quarter as the crow flies from Windsor Castle to Royal Lodge. From the Cambridge Gate of the Castle a mile of road runs through Windsor Great Park, to a statue of George III on horseback. This mile is called the Long Walk. It stretches like a ribbon lined on either side with elms planted by Charles II.

At Royal Lodge, court etiquette was forgotten, and ceremony left behind. We were just a family again. We had all meals together, and went for picnics, and above all, we gardened. The whole place had become overgrown and neglected, and the King decided we would start from scratch. So every Saturday afternoon we all of us put on old clothes. The chauffeur, the butler, even the detective, were all roped in. What His Majesty did at all, he did with all his might, ignoring human frailty. He was an absolute slave-driver, hacking, sawing, pulling out dead wood, heaping up bonfires. Many there were who would willingly have fallen out for a

The Royal Family in their magnificent Coronation robes

12 May 1937. The Princesses follow the King in the Coronation procession at Westminster Abbey

From the balcony of Buckingham Palace, the Royal Family acknowledge the acclamation of the waiting crowds

A break from lessons for a trip on the Thames

A pony show held at London's Agricultural Hall is the spectacle that so engrosses Princess Margaret's attention

The Princesses at Royal Lodge about to set out for a morning ride

On a voyage downriver in a PLA launch, Princess Margaret uses the ship's microphone. Her message to the royal party was: 'We are going to have some tea in a minute!'

Balmoral Castle

Something catches Princess Margaret's eye. She pauses in her work, and looks up with mingled interest and amusement

In the garden of Royal Lodge, Windsor

Princess Elizabeth did not find knitting easy. But on this occasion she seems well satisfied with the result of her efforts

Princess Margaret, with her purchase in her hand, leaving a bazaar held at Crathie Church

After watching a Welsh Pit Ponies' Display, the Princesses were presented with silver replicas of miners' lamps. Here, Princess Margaret hurries back to the royal box to show her gift to the Queen

Princess Elizabeth sits for sculptor K. S. de Strobl, while Crawfie looks on

The Royal Family at Portsmouth where the King and
Queen embarked for their visit to Canada and the USA

*A studio portrait of Princess Margaret,
aged eight and a half years*

*The Princesses, with Crawfie, aboard the destroyer that took them
to meet the King and Queen on their return from Canada and the USA*

Princess Elizabeth life-saving during a competition at the Bath Club, London

Marion Crawford

At a dress rehearsal of the Aldershot Tattoo, Princess Elizabeth
has a point in the programme explained to her

The Royal Family join in the community singing
during an August 1939 visit to the King's Camp at Abergeldie

The Princesses join forces to solve their outsize jig-saw puzzle

Princess Elizabeth rehearses her broadcast to the children of England

The Princesses 'get down' to a card game in the schoolroom at Windsor

Princess Elizabeth at work on her lessons in the schoolroom at Windsor Castle

Princess Margaret busies herself with her paints

Fourteen-year-old Prince Philip dressed for his part in a school performance of Macbeth

Princess Margaret, a keen pianist, practises at Windsor Castle

When this picture of the Princesses in their pony cart at Windsor was first released to the Press it was described as 'taken in the garden of the country residence where they are staying during the war'

A small companion in attendance, Princess Margaret relaxes with a book

rest and a breather. How could we, when the King was still working away?

The Queen was always in rather a panic on these occasions. I can still hear her saying in anguish, 'Darling! Darling, do mind ... Lilibet, get out of the way ... Margaret, for goodness sake, look where you are going.'

For these occasions the oldest possible tweeds, stockings, and gloves came out, and wisely, for we were in constant danger from trailing brambles. The King had a wonderful collection of tree-cutting implements which were always a source of worry to the Queen and an attraction to the children. They were so sharp that you bled if you looked at them.

The smell of wood smoke, the crackling of bonfires, will always remind me poignantly of those days. As will blisters on the inside of the hand!

For the King, alas, the fun now ended at teatime. There was no more after-tea hide-and-seek, no happy romps about the passages. The Parliamentary boxes came. These large black-leather boxes contain the papers of the day's doings in Parliament, sent up by the ministers. They come by dispatch rider, and keep the King informed as to what has been going on during the day. His own secretaries send up household documents that need attention at the same time.

I sometimes wondered whether he had the two life-sized rocking-horses placed outside his study door on purpose, so that he could hear the thump, thump of the little girls riding them while he worked, and could feel them still near him.

CHAPTER V

Royal Occasions

IN the early months of his rule the King appeared to me to grow taller, though I don't suppose he really did. It was an astonishing experience to see this very youthful person, who had always been the self-effacing and delicate one of the family, come into his own.

Lilibet and Margaret left for Scotland for the holiday they looked forward to all the year round. It tended to be the chief landmark in their calendar. Things were apt to date from 'before we went to Scotland' or 'when we got back from Scotland'. But now it was no longer the small, comfortable Birkhall they went to. It was Balmoral Castle itself. They knew it, having often visited their grandparents there, but it had seemed until then just a place to visit, not one to stay in.

The Castle stands in a wonderful position in the Dee Valley, close to Braemar, surrounded by famous grouse moors and hills that were planted with Scottish firs by order of Queen Victoria. It is an ancient baronial castle with a keep and many towers with winding stairways and small unhandy rooms in them difficult to furnish.

The drawing room and dining room have been modernized by the King and Queen, but upstairs everything is much as Queen Victoria left it. Tartan linoleum, tartan curtains, and bedroom china of the old-fashioned basin-and-jug type, and even little hair tidies made of tartan hang on dressing-mirrors. Landseers predominate, mostly prints. One way and another, we all got sated with Landseers at Balmoral, but there was more to come. Before we left London that first year, I had arranged that we should have one of the beautiful pictures from the picture galleries brought up to the schoolroom every week, to give the children a chance to study it. There were so many of them that they got overlooked and lost in the crowd. Imagine our chagrin when we returned to the London school-room and found that our week's picture was 'Dignity and Impudence' – by Landseer.

In the drawing room at Balmoral there is a collection of paintings of heads of past gillies, or hunting servants, all look-ing immensely patriarchal. A full-sized statue of the Prince Consort stands for ever in the front hall, with a patient and slightly martyred expression, as though he was getting a little tired of waiting around.

Everyone loves to go to Balmoral. There is always much conjecture among the staff, as to who will be taken and who left. The staff bedrooms are all up at the top of the Castle, looking over the hills. The men are on one side, the women carefully segregated on the other side – another relic of the Victorian regime. It is very quiet all winter, up there in the hills. But with the arrival of the Royal Family, the whole countryside comes to life again. The little church of Crathie is packed every Sunday, and a great outburst of social life suc-ceeds the empty months of winter and spring.

When October came, we could hear the stags roaring in the hills. Sometimes, from afar, we watched them fighting. We were always horrified at the faithlessness of the females, who stood meekly around to see who won, and then lined up behind the winner. No one, it seemed, ever stood by the poor stag who had been vanquished and cast out.

Meals were simple but substantial. Everyone ate more,

because of the cold. Sir Harold Campbell, one of the equerries, went into the kitchens himself to show the English cooks how porridge ought to be made. The Royal Family always brought their cooks up with them.

Tea, a meal for which Scotland has always been famous, became one of the high spots of the day. There would be shrimps, hot sausage-rolls, scones, and those various sorts of griddle cakes known in Scotland as baps and bannocks. This meal was laid out on a table in the drawing room, where everyone automatically collected as soon as the men who had been out with the guns came down from the moors.

In the evenings there would probably be a cinema show, which would be attended by all the staff and household, and maybe some of the estate people would come in for it as well. The films always had to be carefully chosen. The Scottish country people are very strict and upright, and disapprove of anything that could come under the heading of 'carryings on'.

At night, after dinner, seven pipers in their kilts and sporrans would walk playing through the hall and the dining room. At one time they were all sergeant-majors, and it was considered a great honour to be one of the chosen pipers to pipe for the King. His Majesty still has a personal piper who goes around with him, and who at one time did nothing at all but pipe. Since the war, however, he has had to take a hand with the waiting at table.

Lilibet and Margaret loved this nightly ceremony and were usually waiting to peep over the stairs at the seven stalwart pipers going by. They looked down on to the top of them.

There was a regiment on guard at the Castle, but they were not too obvious. The young officers loved to play sardines, musical chairs, or hide-and-seek with the children, and later on came in very handy for dances and other games. One annual function was the Gillies' Ball. Yearly this is given for the King's outdoor staff and their wives and families.

The King and Queen always opened the ball with the oldest members of the party. When Lilibet was twelve she was allowed to come down for a little while for the first time and take part in some of the reels. She did not wear any special frock, just a little-girl party dress.

Lilibet was far more strictly disciplined than Margaret ever was. Margaret was having quite a lot of social life from the age of ten onward. But the King set a very high standard for Lilibet, perhaps because she is heir to the throne. Margaret was a great joy and a diversion, but Lilibet had a kind of natural grace all her own. The King had great pride in her, and she in turn had an inborn desire to do what was expected of her.

The children had few friends outside their own family circle, and apart from one occasion never seemed to feel the need of them. Only once did Lilibet make rather special friends with a little girl in London. They played together in Hamilton Gardens, and I felt there was real attraction between them. When they grew older the other child was sent away to school and the friendship came to an untimely end. It is a pity, for it might have been a very pleasant relationship. This was the only young girl Lilibet ever appeared to rather single out for herself and feel drawn to. She was Sonia Graham Hodgson, daughter of Dr H.K. Graham Hodgson (now Sir Harold), CVO, the eminent radiologist who has X-rayed four generations of the Royal Family.

Lilibet's first love of all was undoubtedly Owen the groom, who taught her to ride. What Owen did or said was right in her sight for many years, and I remember how we all laughed on one occasion when she asked her father about some future plan that was being made.

'Don't ask me, ask Owen,' said the King, a trifle testily. 'Who am I to make suggestions?'

❉

It was now that dress was to become for me a very serious problem. I would have my budget made out and my year's outfit planned, then some royal personage would die, plunging the court into mourning, and myself into a quandary. In Edward VII's time the Palace staff got their mourning provided, but this convenient arrangement had lapsed before I went there.

There was never, in the Palace, much chance to wear out old clothes, as I had to be prepared to go out at short notice. One of the children would come with a message: 'Mummie is taking us to the National Gallery, Crawfie, and she would like you to come with us.' I would have perhaps two minutes to get ready. One cannot keep the Queen waiting.

There were now balls and splendid parties, and the wardrobe that had been adequate at 145 Piccadilly no longer sufficed. I can still remember the thrill of my first State ball, and the frantic preparations I made for it. I had a saxe-blue velvet dress with a wide skirt and simple bodice, and a cluster of artificial roses of all shades which cost me a small fortune. They were made in France. I wore a pink taffeta petticoat which rustled and made me feel very splendid. I was ready much too soon and felt sick with excitement. There came a knock at my door, and a little figure in a dressing-gown came in. It was Margaret.

'Oh, Crawfie,' she said, 'you look lovely! Are you excited?'

Indeed I was. For many years, before balls, or Courts, or parties, Margaret would come to my room like this, I admiring her, she admiring me. But this special evening has always remained with me because it was the first. And it was made quite perfect for me, because the King himself asked me to dance.

Lilibet was bridesmaid for the first time to her uncle, the Duke of Kent, and his beautiful young wife. He was the best-looking of all the Princes, and they certainly made a glamorous couple. Marina was a fairy-story princess come to life, and I have never forgotten how lovely I thought her when I first saw her.

Contrary to common gossip that went around about these two, theirs was also a love match and not a marriage for reasons of State. Nor was she (another popular story) originally intended for his brother, the Duke of Windsor. The young Duke of Kent met her and fell in love with her. They had a lot in common. The Duke was very musical, and like his mother, Queen Mary, he had great knowledge of pictures and old china. He was extremely artistic and took a hand in the planning of their home.

It was about this time that another young man first appeared on the scene from time to time, I remember. This was Mr Norman Hartnell, whom we all came to know so well. In those days he was young and slim, and perhaps just a little intense. He fitted Lilibet's brides maid's frock for the Kent wedding and stood back to admire the general effect, one hand on his hip. Margaret, then a small girl, was immensely intrigued by him.

Mr Hartnell has made most of the Queen's clothes ever since. It was he who designed Lilibet's very beautiful wedding dress.

Both the King and Queen wanted to have their daughters feel they were, as far as possible, members of the community. Just how difficult this is to achieve, if you live in a palace, is hard to explain. A glass curtain seems to come down between you and the outer world, between the hard realities of life and those who dwell in a court, and however hard a struggle is made to avoid it, escape is not entirely possible. This strange atmosphere is not engendered by royalty itself. Often royalty fights very hard in an endeavour to keep in touch with the world as it is.

I myself had never ceased striving to keep this miasma of unreality from the children, and thanks to their parents' open-mindedness in these matters, I often succeeded.

I suggested one day that it would be a very good idea for the children to start a Girl Guide company at the Palace. Besides keeping them in touch with what children of their own ages were doing, I knew it would bring them into contact with others of their own ages and of all kinds and conditions.

Both the King and the Queen were extremely helpful and encouraging. No one ever worked for more helpful and appreciative employers.

We got hold of Miss Violet Synge – later to become Guide Commissioner for all England. At first she was a trifle appalled at the idea. She did not see how it could possibly work.

One of my greatest difficulties always was to get people to realize that these two little girls wanted only to be treated as any other normal and healthy little girls of their own ages.

'How could it ever answer?' Miss Synge said. 'Guides must all treat one another like sisters.'

I had some difficulty in persuading her that there was nothing Lilibet and Margaret would like better than to be treated like sisters, for in those days they were quite ready to take the whole world to their hearts.

'Come and meet them and talk it over,' I suggested.

So Miss Synge came to tea. She found two polite and very enthusiastic little girls. One difficulty there was. Margaret was too young to be a Guide. This bothered Lilibet immensely.

'You don't think we could get her in somehow?' she asked. 'She is very strong, you know. Pull up your skirts, Margaret, and show Miss Synge. You can't say those aren't a very fine pair of hiking legs, Miss Synge. And she loves getting dirty, don't you, Margaret, and how she would love to cook sausages on sticks.'

So persuasive was Lilibet that in the end we got round the difficulty by arranging to have two Brownies attached to the Palace Guides, and making Margaret one of them. Later we started a Brownie company of our own, and the movement grew and was a most popular one. We had twenty Guides and fourteen Brownies, drawn from the children of court officials and those of Palace employees. King George's summerhouse in the garden came in most handy then as our headquarters.

The King made one stipulation only. 'I'll stand anything,' he said, 'but I won't have them wear those hideous long black stockings. Reminds me too much of my youth.'

So the Palace Guides wore knee-length beige stockings instead, and in a short time this innovation was gladly adopted by the Guides everywhere.

The Princess Royal, magnificent in her Guide uniform, came down to enrol everybody. She was a great deal more nervous than the recruits, because the King stood behind her in a doorway looking on, making *sotto voce* brotherly remarks which she found it difficult not to laugh at.

Just at first, some of the children who joined started coming in party frocks, with white gloves, accompanied by fleets of nannies and governesses. We soon put a stop to all that.

There was one Guide game we played where all the shoes are heaped together in the middle of the room, and their owners have to find their own, put them on, and see who can get back to the starting-line first. This never went very well, as quite half the children did not know their own shoes! Lilibet and Margaret told me this with scorn. There was never any nonsense of that kind in *their* nursery.

Lilibet was growing up. She was now thirteen. At this age, when so many are gawky, she was an enchanting child with the loveliest hair and skin and a long, slim figure. There was still no official mention made of her being heir to the throne.

It must not be overlooked that for some time after the accession there was still the chance that one day there might come along 'a brother for Margaret and Lilibet'. Was this a disappointment to the King and Queen? I never knew. But as time went on and it seemed more than likely Lilibet would one day be Queen, we felt her education should proceed on wider lines than before.

The Queen spoke to Sir Jasper Ridley about this one day. She told him that she would like Sir Henry Marten to take Princess Elizabeth in Constitutional History. Sir Henry Marten was then Vice-Provost of Eton College and an eminent scholar. From then on I took Princess Elizabeth twice a week to Sir Henry at Eton, until the war started, when he came to Windsor Castle.

Sir Henry Marten was a charming person, learned and erudite but extremely human. He had a round, smooth, full face and a bald head, and a habit of chewing one corner of his handkerchief and gazing at the ceiling when he was thinking. He loved sweet things, and always had a few lumps of sugar in his pocket. During the war, when Lilibet had lots of honey from abroad, she sent him two pounds every week.

We went over to Eton College for the lessons. They took place in his study. Lilibet had been a little overawed at the prospect, and she clung to my arm as we went up the stairs. In the study there wasn't a chair to sit on. Books everywhere. Piles of books stood like stalagmites on the floor.

'Crawfie, do you mean to tell me he has read them *all*?' Lilibet gasped. It filled her with deep admiration for him, I think.

Then the door opened and he came in and shook hands with her in his courteous fashion, at once making her feel grown-up and important. Far from being the dusty-looking figure one expected in a scholar, he appeared to me to be rather dapper.

Lilibet, who had been very shy, felt entirely at home with him, and there was a real and rather charming friendship between the little girl and the old scholar. I sat in the window during the lessons.

'Like a book to read, Miss Crawford?' said Sir Henry. He handed me the latest Wodehouse, *Uncle Fred in the Springtime*.

Meanwhile, over the courtyard the boys came and went, wearing that strange Eton uniform, a silk top hat and short coat and white bow tie and striped dark trousers, that always suggests a gathering of adolescent undertakers. Some of the hats, no doubt belonging to the dandies among them, were immaculately brushed and burnished, but the greater number looked rather dusty.

Their manners were charming. From time to time one would come in with a message or to fetch a book. They would bow to me and to the little girl seated at the table, but pay no other attention to us, though they must have known very well who she was. As we came and went, never once were we the centre of curiosity. The boys would raise their ruffled toppers politely, go about their business, and leave us to ours.

Not very long after we moved into the Palace the King had a very badly poisoned hand. When he was better, his doctors advised him to go to the sea for a while to convalesce. So it came about that the two little Princesses got what for most children is an annual event, and went to the seaside. They had never been there together before, free to dig and paddle and ride on the sands.

The Duke of Devonshire lent the King his house near Eastbourne. It is called Compton Place, and is a lovely big, square house just under the Sussex Downs. The family took their own staff there with them, with the exception of the gardeners. The Queen took her personal maid, the King his valet, and we took our own housemaids who looked after us. Also our own detectives.

Mr Cameron and Mr Giles were the two detectives. Whenever the car went out, one of them sat in front with the driver, ready to be helpful if there was any unexpected hold-up, or if crowds gathered, or the situation got in any way out of hand. They had to come along even when the family went for a picnic. Mr Cameron was simply marvellous. We used to laugh about him and say he must have an invisible cloak. As soon as the car stopped he just faded into the landscape.

The detectives' job was to see everything worked smoothly. They saw the local inspectors of police every morning and gave them a rough idea of what the King and Queen would be doing, and where they would be likely to be. This was especially necessary on a Sunday when the family went to church, and the crowds, unless controlled, could not be relied on to be reasonable.

It was springtime. The country was looking beautiful. The King and Queen enjoyed this unexpected spell of freedom. They took us out from time to time for that greatest treat of all, tea in an hotel. It was usually served upstairs in a private room. Otherwise it would have been the old story of crowds gathering.

The little girls rode ponies on the sands, and we built sand castles and collected shells. In the evenings the King and Queen would walk together in the beautiful gardens, arm in arm. It was pleasant to see them together. They were still much in love.

The King, when he was alone with his family, was boyish and full of fun. One day while we were at Eastbourne, he very solemnly handed me a matchbox.

'It's a present for you, Crawfie,' he said.

I opened it with interest, and found it contained my pet abomination, green sand worms!

At Compton Place there was a large table in the hall on which was always kept a jig-saw puzzle of some thousands of pieces. Anyone waiting around or with a moment to spare would have a go at it. The two little girls became quite expert at this. They were both very neat-fingered and good and quick at picking up anything new.

At one time I got quite anxious about Lilibet and her fads. She became almost too methodical and tidy. She would hop out of bed several times a night to get her shoes quite straight, her clothes arranged just so. We soon laughed her out of this. I remember one hilarious session we had with Margaret imitating her sister going to bed. It was not the first occasion, or the last, on which Margaret's gift of caricature came in very handy.

Long before most children do, Lilibet took an interest in politics, and knew quite a bit of what was going on in the world outside. She was always deeply interested in people, and I think Sir Henry Marten's instruction fostered this interest, and taught her that all history has to do with people and not with a lot of dummies who have little or no relation to ourselves.

The King also would talk to his elder daughter more seriously than most fathers do to so young a child, and I was often very much touched and impressed by the way he did it. It was as if he spoke to an equal. Since he had become King the shadows were closing in on England. They were, I think, realized in the Palace a long time before they fell over the streets outside.

Meanwhile there were the garden parties to which the little girls now began to go with Mummie and Papa. For these occasions they wore very simple afternoon frocks – these were usually of tussore silk, often hand-smocked, quite short, with knickers to match – and straw hats and white cotton socks.

They were never in the least interested in what they were going to wear and just put on what they were told. People liked to see them at these affairs, but I don't think the children much enjoyed them.

Three thousand people (nowadays six thousand) are always asked to the garden parties. They crowd the gardens and concentrate upon the King and Queen. The little girls, being small at that time, must have suffered from lack of air in all that crush, especially on a hot day. I personally always avoided these parties. I had a far better time sitting in the window of my room with a tea tray and a pair of field-glasses.

The family always split up into parties and move around among their guests, being affable to everyone and saying a word to this person and that. It is always a great joy to them to recognize a face they know. They make their way across the lawns to an enclosed space where they have their own tea pavilion and entertain members of the diplomatic corps and any special guests.

The King and Queen personally go through the whole list of those invited, and select those they wish to be invited into the private enclosure. Should they come across the names of a miner and his wife who have been asked perhaps because of record-breaking in the pits, or an airwoman who has made a distinguished journey, or someone who has lately won a tournament, the Members of the Household are instructed to find them and bring them along to be presented to Their Majesties. Anybody who has gained distinction in any walk of life may be singled out in this way.

Both the little girls used to breathe a sigh of relief when they at last got through the crowds and came into the enclosure. Meanwhile Queen Mary would be going round by another route, smiling and greeting her friends and anyone else that she happened to recognize.

Queen Mary is always a most popular figure at these

parties. She, too, finally arrives at the royal enclosure. The first time Lilibet and Philip appeared in public together was at one of these parties, where, like any other newly-engaged girl, Lilibet went round proudly showing her new engagement ring.

At the last garden party which my husband and I attended, the chief figure round whom everyone flocked and who got the royal welcome of the day was not a member of the family at all. It was Winston Churchill. He came down the steps from the Bow Room into the garden to find a royal reception waiting for him. A path had been cleared for him through the crowds, and everyone clapped and fought to shake his hand or pat his shoulder. So this grand old warrior made his way over the garden to have tea with the King.

At six o'clock a gentle hint that it is time to go home is given when the band plays the National Anthem. The family form a procession and go back to the Palace. I remember being very amused once, hearing Lilibet instruct Margaret before they went down to one of these parties as to how she must behave.

'And if you do see someone with a funny hat, Margaret, you must *not* point at it and laugh,' she told her sister solemnly, 'and you must *not* be in too much of a hurry to get through the crowds to the tea table. That's not polite either.'

The main event of the London season had always been the Courts at which the year's debutantes would be presented to the King and Queen. These were far more formal than the garden parties.

People cannot apply for an invitation to a Court as they can to a garden party, which confers no social distinction whatever. Debutantes must be presented by their mothers or by someone who herself has the entrée. Each girl must be presented again on her marriage, in her new name. These can then in their turn present to the King and Queen their own children, or others of their circle, but they are required to be entirely responsible for them.

Official dress was always worn at the Courts. This gives to the whole evening an air of glamour. The men wear knee breeches and silk stockings, tailed coats and medals and orders. The women wear full evening dress, and five-foot trains. In their hair they have three curled ostrich feathers, and a long white tulle veil hanging down behind. The King and Queen, wearing their crowns and very beautiful jewels, sit side by side on two thrones, the other members of the family present grouped behind them with their equerries and ladies-in-waiting.

Those to be presented pass in front of Their Majesties and make their curtsies as their names are called out by the Lord Chamberlain. All this is done to soft music played by a band of one of the Guards regiments in a gallery above the Throne Room. Ushers with long rods sweep up the ladies' trains for them, and throw them skilfully over the owner's arm when the curtsy is finished.

There was always a feeling of excitement in the Palace on the night of a Court. The little girls in their dressing-gowns used to peep through the windows at the crowds of cars, the beautiful ladies and the Gentlemen-at-Arms, wearing their plumed hats, arriving.

'We have a fly's-eye view,' Lilibet said.

The high spot of the evening was when they went down to see their mother and father dressed and ready to make their entrance. Other members of the family came along also in their Court finery. We always waited with real excitement to see what Aunt Marina, the Duchess of Kent, would be wearing. For she was one of the loveliest of them all.

I remember particularly one dress of hers. It was white brocade with pink and silver flowers embossed on it, very simply made as a background for her magnificent jewels. She wore a diamond-and-ruby tiara and a diamond-and-ruby necklace, which her husband had given her, and I have never seen anyone look more lovely.

Both the little girls admired her immensely and they took a passionate interest in her hats.

'When I am grown up,' Margaret said, 'I shall dress like Aunt Marina does.' She told me that one day when she was about ten, and it is a promise she has tried hard to keep.

I always found the Duchess of Kent a very attractive person. Personally an exceptionally beautiful woman, she is natural, home-loving, and domesticated. In those days, in the heyday of her youth and beauty, her home and children always came first with her. I often went over to Coppins during the war. This was then her country house, and is now her permanent home. The Duchess has three children: Prince Edward, the present Duke of Kent, a schoolboy at Eton; Princess Alexandra, at boarding-school in Ascot; and Prince Michael, her youngest. He was seven weeks old when his father was killed.

She always bathed the baby herself. I used to go over and watch her sometimes, and think what a pretty picture she made with the little boy.

Prince Philip is her cousin. They both have that clean-cut Viking look.

In their pink quilted dressing-gowns, with rosebud pattern, the little girls would then watch the royal procession form to enter the Throne Room. We could hear the music from the band faint and far away, and we looked down on a sea of waving white ostrich feathers worn by the ladies in their hair.

'Never mind, Margaret,' Lilibet said comfortingly, 'one day you and I will be down there sharing all the fun. And I shall have a perfectly *enormous* train, yards long.'

It was always a little difficult to get them to bed on these nights, for it was long after midnight before the last car started up, the last coach clattered out of the courtyard, and silence fell.

In the spring of 1939 the King and Queen went to Canada and the United States. I was left with the two Princesses at Buckingham Palace. There had been some talk of our going to Marlborough House to be under Queen Mary's grandmotherly eye, but I was glad when the final decision was to leave us in our familiar quarters. It made less of an upheaval, and I felt the children would feel their parents' absence to be merely a temporary affair that way.

The actual departure had been rather slurred over in all the excitement of the packing and of inspecting Mummie's pretty new clothes.

The Queen always has to take a great deal of luggage on these official trips. Dozens of evening frocks are necessary to cope with the differing climates and places in which she must appear. All these are packed by her maids, who are known as dressers. They have complete charge of her whole wardrobe. She must also take hats, bags, gloves, shoes for every outfit.

Two dressers always travel with her, and she takes a lady-in-waiting who also acts as her secretary. The King takes his valet, a detective – usually the ubiquitous Mr Cameron – and a couple of secretaries. Sir Piers Legh accompanied them to Canada as equerry. He arranged all the social functions, and so on. He was up in all the odd details of court etiquette, which are pretty complicated but not entirely meaningless, and could pass them on to people wanting to entertain the King and Queen.

Queen Mary took the children down to Portsmouth for the final goodbyes. I think the King and Queen felt the part-

ing more than the children did. They were enchanted by the
train journey and seeing the ships.

I was afraid there might be tears when they got home to the
empty Palace and Mummie' s and Papa's rooms with nobody
in them. But everything went off quite smoothly, and we
began right away to make plans for their parents' return.
Children are always happy when they have something to look
forward to. I had strict injunctions to write often, and give all
details of the children's growth, how they were getting on, and
how many new teeth appeared!

One day there was great excitement. We had a call on the
transatlantic telephone. The voices of the King and Queen
came through so clearly they might have been in the next
room. We ended the conversation by holding the Queen's
corgi, Dookie, up and making him bark down the telephone
by pinching his behind.

He was devoted to the Queen, poor Dookie, but very sour-
natured otherwise. I never knew where he got his name. He
came to the Palace with it, I think. He bit me once quite
severely, and on another occasion took a piece out of Lord
Lothian's hand. With great fortitude his lordship averred it
was nothing! It did not hurt him at all.

'All the same, he bled all over the floor,' Lilibet pointed out.

Meantime, Queen Mary kept an eye on us as she had
promised to do. She is one of the kindest and most consider-
ate of people, and it is not for nothing that most of the staff
in her employ have been there all their lives, and grown old
with her.

She frequently took the children off my hands, 'to give you
a bit of a rest, Crawfie'. This was a wonderful opportunity, she
felt, for packing in some educational visits.

Besides visits to museums, art galleries, the Bank of
England, and the Tower of London, she took us all one day

over the Royal Mint. They were making the King's new seal, which we all inspected, and we saw the money being tied up into bags by machinery.

Another time Mr Montagu Norman took us all over the vaults in the Bank of England. There was the gold, standing packed up all round.

'It looks just like bricks,' said Lilibet, rather disappointed in it. Mr Norman said anyone who could carry one of those bricks away could have it. How hard we tried! Alas, we could not even move one.

David and Michael Bowes-Lyon, the children's uncles, were very kind at this time and took the children off for weekends with them. I did not go because they thought a little rest would be nice for me.

We had hundreds of letters and snapshots from all sorts of people in Canada and the United States along the way the King and Queen travelled. These were often sent anonymously. A stationmaster from some small town in America wrote saying he had seen the King and Queen go through his station, and he was sure the little Princesses would be glad to know they looked well.

A small boy took a snapshot of Their Majesties talking with Indians and squaws, and sent that. People from both countries posted them great bundles of comics, which they loved, to cheer them while their parents were away. Other children wrote to them saying, 'My Mummie and Daddy have been away in India for a long time, so I know what it must feel like for you.'

It was a wonderful experience for the little girls to realize how many kind people there were in the world, and how many unknown friends they had who thought about them and wished them well, and this was the first time it had happened to them.

The King and Queen wrote long letters telling us of their

various trips and of a picnic at Hyde Park. 'But that's just round the corner!' said Margaret, and I had to explain that there was another Hyde Park. The King caused a lot of amusement by saying he had been eating 'hot dogs'.

We meantime settled down to a spell of uninterrupted schoolroom routine, which I for one was glad of. There were a few moments when the Princesses pored wistfully over maps of the United States and thought what a long way off their parents were. But those did not last long. We went to Royal Lodge for weekends, and though here we were rather more conscious of empty rooms and vacant places, the time passed quickly enough.

The two little girls spring-cleaned their Little House, I remember, from top to bottom, shook all the mats, brushed the carpets, and prepared for the home-coming of Mummie and Papa just as the staff were doing at the Palace.

The return was a great event in the children's lives. We got up very early in the morning. Lilibet and Margaret had grown enormously during their parents' absence; some teeth had been lost, and others were half coming. There were four of us – the children, Alah, and myself. We went to Southampton on the train. The children had their comics to read, and people were awfully nice about their going to meet their parents. There were much bigger crowds there for the home-coming at the station, waving into the carriage.

When we got to Southampton we had to go on a destroyer out in mid-Channel to meet the *Empress of Britain*. The destroyer was rather fun. It was all newly painted grey from stern to stern, and the children were terribly thrilled.

When we were on board the Captain said, 'Would you like to stay on deck or go below, or what?' because the vibration was terrific on the destroyer. It was the first time the children had ever been on one.

At eleven o'clock he asked if they would like some hot soup. They looked at him with great horror and said, 'Oh, no thank you!' Alah had retired to the cabin below. I think she was not feeling very well. Then he produced a bowl of lovely cherries, and we stood and ate them on the deck. The destroyer was very clean and so tidy, and we did not know what to do with the cherry stones. We felt we could not be seen throwing them overboard, and so we flung them down one of the ventilation shafts!

Then the *Empress of Britain* came in sight and we went below to tidy. The Captain's cabin amused us, with its, to us, almost primitive amenities. There were photographs of children and a dignified-looking wife.

The steward came to take us on deck, and we saw the *Empress of Britain* heaving to. We had to go down a very precarious ladder to get on the barge. The Captain said, 'Jump when I tell you.' One minute the destroyer was up and the barge was down, and the next moment it was just the reverse.

We got on board safely, however, and Alah also managed to jump when the Captain said 'Jump'. As we approached what seemed a colossal ship, we saw the King and Queen amidships. Then we had to go through the same process again to get on board the *Empress*.

There were these two figures waiting with great eagerness, looking down the stairs as we mounted. The little girls could hardly walk up the ladder quickly enough, for climbing was very awkward, but when they reached the top they rushed to Mummie and Papa. They kissed them and hugged them again and again. Everybody else kept out of the way, and I hesitated halfway up the gangway too. It was a very joyful reunion indeed.

Then I went up and curtsied, and they seemed very pleased to see me. The Queen kissed me and said how much the children had grown and how well they looked, and all the time the

King could hardly take his eyes off Lilibet. I have a photograph which shows the Queen, very slim, holding Margaret's hand, wearing her favourite blue, with grey shoes and stockings and handbag, and the King looking at Lilibet.

Margaret during the period of the Canada-America trip had begun to thin down a bit. She just clung to Mummie's hand, glad to have her back again. She made us all laugh by saying, 'Look, Mummie, I am quite a good shape now, not like a football like I used to be.'

On the big ship we did not notice the swell. We had a hilarious luncheon party with all the officers and members of the household. The Commander-in-Chief of Southampton came out with the welcoming party, and several other Southampton officials.

We had lunch in the ship's dining-room, which we thought extremely ugly. The walls were a horrible pink, the carpet a hoosh-mi of bright colours, and pots of artificial palms were strewn around everywhere. It looked just like a stage set for a musical comedy, and this was enhanced by the fact that they had hung up lots of streamers and balloons, which the little girls, at least, thought were wonderful. Everybody talked nineteen to the dozen, and the children hung round Mummie and Papa, delighted to have them back.

In the exuberance of the moment I drank a champagne cocktail, a thing I seldom do. It had a most odd effect on me, and I suddenly felt very untrustful of my knees, and all the noise seemed suddenly to be coming from a very long way off!

The Queen gave me a sympathetic glance, and laughed. 'Poor Crawfie,' she said, 'I ought to have warned you. They make them rather strong aboard.'

The King threw balloons out of the portholes, Lord Airlie popped some with his cigarette, and everyone was very youthful and gay. I thought the King seemed a little sad when he said goodbye to the ship and the sailors. He had always loved the sea.

Back at the Palace we had the usual crowds and balcony appearances, this time enjoyed by everyone rather more than usual. It had been so long since the King and Queen had been home among their own people.

The children went late to bed that night. There were so many parcels to open, so many tales to tell. People from all over the States and Canada had sent presents to the little girls. Among the things that delighted them most were some frilly American pinafores sent by some children out West, and some small totem poles about a foot high. They were quaintly carved, and coloured Indian fashion. They had them on the mantelshelf in their room for years.

CHAPTER VI

The Outbreak of War

BEFORE the Royal Family went to Balmoral in August there came an incident that was going to have very wide results in everybody's life.

We went for the weekend to Dartmouth on the King's yacht, the *Victoria and Albert*, on a private visit, for the King wanted to visit Dartmouth College. Lilibet was thirteen at this time, and it had been decided to take the Princesses and myself there for a few days.

The *Victoria and Albert* was a delightful yacht. It was very Victorian in decor, with colourful cretonne decorations in the cabins. It was rather roomy above for the family, but I shudder to think of what it was like below where the sailors slept. They must have been packed like sardines.

She is a large gold-and-white yacht with a massive figurehead, beautifully painted. The cabins were still fitted with old-fashioned bunks, but bathrooms had been put in. The two little girls had adjoining cabins. I was at the other end of the yacht, on my own. The King and Queen had cabins amidships.

The children and myself had a very pretty little schoolroom, which was used by Alah for breakfast and tea, and the little girls' supper. But whenever possible, we did lessons out on deck.

The dining saloon gave the children a great thrill, because the yacht's mast came out and up through one end of the dining table. We had very happy parties around this table, and lunch and dinner which we all had together. On private occasions like this, no one could have been pleasanter host and hostess than Their Majesties. We were taught on this occasion by the young officers of the yacht to dance the Lambeth Walk and Palais Glide, a sort of modernized version of some old folk-dance.

The King and Queen took their own chef down with them, and the ship's officers, accustomed to harder tack, enjoyed the change, I think. The weather was good, and we all loved the trip.

The King was holding an inspection at Dartmouth Royal Naval College, where he was himself once a cadet, and for which he has always had a great affection.

The College, which is a vast red-brick building, stands high on a hill looking down on the River Dart. Some nine hundred boys are usually in training there to become naval officers. The College stands among its own playing-fields and farms, and the river affords a good training-ground in the management of boats, and is usually absolutely crawling with them, manned by small boys looking very businesslike in their white sweaters. They do everything at the double, and all orders have to be carried out at a brisk trot. The discipline there is extremely strict, but in no other school do the boys look so well or so happy, and there are very few who have passed through who do not look back on their time at Dartmouth with pleasure.

On the Sunday morning we were going to the College because there was to be a special service. We climbed those long steps at Dartmouth. I remember that it was a lovely day, though it became a bit cloudy at about eleven. Just about the time the service was scheduled to start and the boys had been paraded before the King and Queen, the Dartmouth College doctor said, 'I am very, very sorry, but two of the boys have developed mumps.'

There was a long conversation as to whether the children ought to go into the chapel, and the Queen finally said, 'Crawfie, would you take them into the Dalrymple-Hamiltons' house,' which I did.

The Dalrymple-Hamilton family lived in the Captain's House at Dartmouth College. The house had a very pleasant lived-in feeling, and the children – a boy and a girl rather older than the Princesses – came out to meet us. There was a clockwork railway laid out all over the nursery floor, and we all knelt down to play with it.

We played for ages, and after a time, a fair-haired boy, rather like a Viking, with a sharp face and piercing blue eyes, came in. He was good-looking, though rather off-hand in his manner. He said, 'How do you do,' to Lilibet, and for a while they knelt side by side playing with the trains. He soon got bored with that. We had ginger crackers and lemonade, in which he joined, and then he said, 'Let's go to the tennis courts and have some real fun jumping the nets.'

Off they went. At the tennis courts I thought he showed off a good deal, but the little girls were much impressed.

Lilibet said, 'How good he is, Crawfie. How high he can jump.' She never took her eyes off him the whole time. He was quite polite to her, but did not pay her any special attention. He spent a lot of time teasing plump little Margaret.

When we went back to the yacht for lunch, the fair-haired boy was there. He was near Lilibet, and we all sat around and talked and laughed a good deal. After that we went to see the swimming-pool and then it was time to go back to the yacht again. It had started to rain by this time, and we were a bedraggled little party.

We had a very jolly dinner that night, but Lilibet was not allowed to stay up. We danced the Lambeth Walk and the Palais Glide with the young officers. Next day, the fair-haired boy, who turned out to be Prince Philip of Greece, came to lunch again. All eyes were on him, which he obviously enjoyed. Lilibet asked him, 'What would you like to eat? What would you like?' when it came to tea. The Queen said, 'You must make a really good meal, for I suppose it is your last for the day.' Philip had several platefuls of shrimps, and a banana split, among other trifles. To the little girls, a boy of any kind was always a strange creature out of another world. Lilibet sat, pink-faced, enjoying it all very much. To Margaret, anyone who could eat so many shrimps was a hero.

In the end he had to go back to Dartmouth to his classes.

The time came when we had to sail away. We all said good-bye, and the engines started. It is a tricky business getting out of Dartmouth Harbour. Sir Dudley North was the captain in charge. Finally we got well out into the Channel. All the boys from Dartmouth had been allowed to get any sort of craft they could find – motor-boats, rowing-boats, and so on – and they followed the *Victoria and Albert* quite a long way. Then the King got very alarmed and said to Sir Dudley North, 'It's ridiculous, and most unsafe. You must signal them to go back.'

Most of the boys did go back immediately, and all the others followed shortly except this one solitary figure whom we saw rowing away as hard as he could, who was, of course, Philip. Lilibet took the glasses and had a long look at him. In the end the King said, 'The young fool. He must go back, otherwise we will have to heave to and send him back.'

At last Philip seemed to realize they did want him to go back – they were shouting at him through the megaphone – and he turned back while we gazed at him until he became just a very small speck in the distance.

We never seemed to get really settled again after the Canada-America visit in the spring of 1939. An air of restless anticipation hung around the Palace. Probably we had more idea than most people outside how grim things were. I still remember the cold shiver that went down my spine when I heard Czechoslovakia had been overrun. Mr Chamberlain came more and more often, looking harassed and bothered, and ageing under our eyes.

What, people still asked, was Hitler going to do? Looking back on it, it now seems so obvious that I wonder anyone asked, but we still hoped that some eleventh-hour change would take place. It did, but it wasn't the kind we wanted. Germany made a pact with Russia. From that moment I think we all knew there was darkness ahead.

It was August. London was stifling. People were streaming out of town as usual for their holidays. The Royal Family usually went away at this time to Balmoral, but their departure was delayed, and the children were horrified at the idea they might not get up there at all.

'Who *is* this Hitler, spoiling everything?' Margaret demanded.

I remember trying to give the Princess a painstaking and unbiased character sketch, but it wasn't very easy. We attempted to keep the gathering storm clouds from the children.

It was the one time of the year when the King and Queen got right away from court etiquette and had complete freedom, and they as much as the children always looked forward to this annual trip north. Besides which, for the Queen, it was a return to her own part of the world. I remember everyone was a little grim, not knowing whether they would be able to go or not.

Looking back, I can see it was the end of an epoch, not only for the King and Queen. They had had their anxieties for months, and it had told on both of them. Especially, I thought, on the Queen. Until now she had appeared to me so sweet, so gay and young, and always able to deal with tiresome decisions and awkward problems. Now there were too many unpleasant facts to be faced, too many decisions that must be made immediately, too many nightmare possibilities.

It was decided I had better go for my holiday as usual, and I left on 4 August, leaving the little girls in London. Our goodbyes were sad and strained. We were all of us wondering unhappily what would have happened by the time we were together again. The little girls did not know if they would get up north at all, and they watched my departure with envy.

'Lucky Crawfie. Going to Scotland.'

In the end it was decided they would go as usual, on 7 August. I had a triumphant letter from Margaret. 'Well. We're here!' she wrote.

Alah always went with them and had entire charge of the children while I had my holiday.

They went up on the private train from King's Cross Station to Ballater. This train consists of luggage vans, wagons to take the royal cars, and three sleeping- and dining-coaches for the children and their parents. Up to a few years ago, the train was the original one built for Queen Victoria, and was not particularly up to date. The King has since had the dining-car rearranged so that there is now a table in the centre where everyone can sit around. Before, it was just arranged like any other restaurant car on a train.

The Queen has a bedroom and a small sitting room; the King has a bedroom and shares the Queen's sitting room. The children shared a sleeping-car with Alah and Bobo, the nurse-maid, who had a small compartment curtained off. This business of going to bed in the train was always a very exciting one.

The journey took in all about fourteen hours, as the royal train did not allow speed to interfere with comfort. At Ballater the party was met by cars and did the remaining nine miles or so by road.

The children's ponies were sent on ahead by ordinary horse-box. Their endless dogs, including the Queen's bad-tempered Dookie, went with them.

Little they dreamed how long it would be before they saw London again.

War was declared on 3 September. I was still on my holiday when I got a telegram asking if I could come as soon as possible to Birkhall. I collected my things and caught my train for Birkhall, wondering what was going to happen.

It was a gloomy journey. All about Aberdeen station anxious knots of people stood talking. The blackout had started and already shed its gloom over half the country. The station lights had all gone out, and darkened trains were already taking off the young men.

When I arrived at Birkhall I found the King and Queen had already gone south in great haste the night before. The Honourable Mrs Geoffrey Bowlby, the Queen's lady-in-waiting, had stayed for two or three days until such time as I could get there.

The two little girls and Alah were waiting for me. They were anxious and very apprehensive about their parents.

'Why had Mummie and Papa to go back, Crawfie? Do you think the Germans will come and get them?' Margaret asked me.

I remember assuring her heartily that there wasn't the slightest chance of it. I have wondered since why it was that I felt so absolutely confident, but I did. Lilibet was very calm and helpful, as usual, and at once ranged herself on the side of law and order.

'I don't think people should talk about battles and things in front of Margaret,' she said. 'We don't want to upset her.'

The King and Queen telephoned through to us every night at six o'clock. The children waited anxiously for the telephone bell to ring. Then there would be a mad rush. The Queen always had a word with me first. I think they felt it very keenly that at this distressing time the family had to be separated. Both the Queen and the King were most anxious that the children should be kept as far as possible away from it all.

'Stick to the usual programme as far as you can, Crawfie. We don't know what is coming, of course, but carry on as long as possible, just as usual.'

Up there among the moors and heather it was easy to do this. The heather was coming out, and the moors all about us were wine-red and beautiful. The River Muick rippled merrily through the gardens just as usual in those lovely autumn days, while Poland was being overrun and 'lights were going out all over Europe'.

Up here in the Highlands all was peace. The curlews called. The grouse raised its familiar old cry, 'Go back, go back', unharried for once by the guns which were all employed elsewhere.

There was now no Mummie and Papa to visit in the early morning, so they both came to me very punctually at half-past nine. We worked until eleven o'clock, then had our usual break, coffee and biscuits for me, orange juice and biscuits for the little girls. Then we used to catch George, the pony, and saddle him and go for a brisk walk, the children taking it in turns to ride. Everything smelled good, so clean and sweet, and our feet sank deliciously into the moss on either side of the river.

The children and I had lunch together with Sir Basil Brooke, who was in charge of the household up there. The little girls were always rather sad, missing Mummie and Papa, and conscious of the empty places.

I read the newspapers to the children after tea, trying as far as possible to give them some idea of what was happening without too many horrible details. Hitler seemed to be marching all over the place, and I remember Lilibet saying anxiously:

'Oh dear, Crawfie, I hope he won't come over here.'

I said I considered it unlikely, but if he did so, no doubt he would be dealt with. We read of sirens sounding in London, and I tried to explain what they were.

We had just been reading 'At a Solemn Musick', by Milton, in which the line appears, 'Blest pair of sirens, pledges of heaven's joy', and I had some difficulty in making them realize the idea wasn't quite the same, and this was a new kind of siren entirely unblessed. We all laughed a great deal about it.

One night over the wireless we suddenly got the horrible news that brought us slap up against reality. A grave voice regretfully announced the sinking of the battleship *Royal Oak*. We were continually studying *Jane's Fighting Ships*, and the little girls took a personal interest in every one of them. Lilibet jumped horrified from her chair, her eyes blazing with anger. I can still hear her little voice:

'Crawfie, it can't be! All those nice sailors.'

As the situation worsened it was no longer possible to keep things from them. Sometimes tuning in on the radio in the evening we would come all unawares on 'Lord Haw-Haw', the infamous Irishman, William Joyce. Most of his efforts were greeted by the two little girls with peals of laughter, but sometimes when he was more than usually offensive the children would throw books and cushions at the wireless so violently I had to turn it off. There was something oddly arresting about that dreadful voice. Some evenings up in Scotland it was almost impossible to get away from it. Wherever you tuned in, there he was.

As far as the lessons were concerned, this was an interlude I was glad of. There were no interruptions during those quiet days. The children were never called away. Sir Henry Marten set Lilibet history papers, and sent her up notes. She wrote essays for him which I posted down to be corrected.

But I began to find having both the little girls on my hands for lessons all the time was becoming rather much for me. I had to prepare, the night before, lessons for two children, both of different ages, both extremely bright. It was pretty hard work. So presently I got Mrs Montaudon-Smith, whom they both liked, and called Monty, to come and take them in French. We rearranged the school programmes and divided the time, so that I could take each child for a little while every day alone.

Monty was very keen on singing. She taught the children French duets which they sang together so charmingly. This was arranged and practised to be a surprise for Papa and Mummie when they were all together again.

We organized war work. Everyone else was occupied in some way, and the little girls could not wait to do their share. So I organized a large sewing party to meet every Thursday afternoon in the schoolroom at Birkhall.

For these gatherings Alah was hostess. We gave them all tea, sandwiches, drop scones (a sort of Scotch pancake) and jam, and fruitcake. Rationing and shortages had not begun. Later, when they did, everyone had to bring her own sugar with her. Some of them would also contribute a cake or a bake of scones.

The crofters' wives, farmers' wives, wives of estate employees came. Everyone save the residents had long since left.

When, later, evacuees from Glasgow were sent out to the village, their mothers also joined us. The King opened up Craigowan, a large house on the Balmoral estate, for evacuees, where they lived in positively ducal surroundings. Alas, very few appreciated it. The children were terrified of the silence, scared to go into the woods, and frightened if they saw a deer. They were not noticeably clean, and I think the conditions of some of these people came as a great shock to our honest God-fearing country people.

It is impossible to explain the immense difference this stay among country people had on some of the town dwellers who had up till then never seen anything save the slums of large towns. So many of them loved it and appreciated it. But some there were who wanted to take the next bus back to Glasgow. 'Oh, the awful quiet!' they said.

These weekly meetings were very popular in the district. Lilibet and Margaret handed round teacups and cake, and talked away happily to the various women, asking fondly after their departed sons and fathers. They also played gramophone records for the sewing ladies on an old-fashioned horn gramophone that blared so loudly we had already put six scarves down the horn to try to deaden it.

Margaret's favourite tune was Gigli, singing 'Your Tiny Hand is Frozen', which was astonishingly apt as we had only one small cosy stove in the centre of the room, and the weather was very chilly.

Aberdeenshire is the country of the Gordon Highlanders, and most of them are recruited there. Already most of the manses and farms had an empty place. One by one the gardeners and the keepers began to disappear. Weeds sprang up where before no weeds had been seen. The housemaids would sadly tell us of this or that male relative whisked away. Soon out-of-doors one old man would be doing the work of the two or three younger ones who had gone.

One of the things the children loved to do was to go to the nearby Canadian lumber camp which had been opened up to get timber for the war effort. It was a wonderful organization, like an entire new village sprung up outside Ballater on the King's estate. The bulldozers never ceased to fill us with horror and fascination, tearing down our beloved pines. The Canadians would pause in their work to grin at the two little girls with their pony. Two or three of them looked rather like red Indians to us, and for them the Princesses had a particularly warm spot in their hearts and would look out for them.

They moved hundreds of trees a day and sawed them up, and had them sent off to the south. Meantime, in our own woods at Birkhall, one old man with one old horse would take several days to drag out one old tree for the same good cause, or as firewood for the house.

Beyond an occasional trip to the dentist in Aberdeen, the children had few outings, and so these trips took on the air of great treats. There was no bombing up there. We seemed to be at the moment in a different and more peaceful world.

The beautiful autumn days passed and brought the first white frosts on the stubble fields. The hares, golden brown all summer, began to put on their winter coats of white. The wild geese began to come down to the rivers and streams again. We had to begin to think about Christmas, but not with the usual pleasure and excitement, as none of us knew what was going to happen.

The children had never been up in Scotland so late before. They were amazed at our north-country frosts, so much whiter and heavier than the southern ones, and how the whole landscape is suddenly transformed into a magic fairyland by the early falls of snow. They loved the frost patterns on the morning windows, and the bright sun on the white landscapes.

There was no central heating in our bedrooms at Birkhall, and the water in the drinking carafes was often frozen hard, together with the children's sponges and flannels, which delighted them immensely. They were never daunted by things like this and made nothing at all of discomforts.

Just before Christmas I felt we should make some sort of preparation, so I took them to Woolworth's in Aberdeen, where we did some brisk shopping and invested in the sixpenny china ornaments and brooches which usually made the bulk of their Christmas shopping.

The children had to go to the dentist fairly regularly. Lilibet had to wear a series of rubber bands, which meant many visits to the dentist with Alah.

Lilibet and Margaret joined the local Girl Guide company. Meetings took place in the Village Hall. We arranged hikes and tea parties and outings, bringing in the evacuees. All this helped to keep the children from missing their parents too much. We still did not know whether we would be marooned in Scotland over Christmas or not, so I thought we had best make plans. It snowed, which seemed to make Christmas very near.

Various people came up for weekends while we were in Scotland, and we had great fun with them. I still have a rather touching letter written me by one of them thanking me for my kindness and patience – for he was an old man at the time. He was devoted to Lilibet, and I remember him watching her one day, and remarking to me, 'There is England's future hope.'

But he was frightened of Margaret. Old men often were. She had too witty a tongue and too sharp a way with her, and I think they one and all felt they would probably be the next on her list of caricatures!

Poor little Margaret. This misunderstanding of her light-hearted fun and frolics was often to get her into trouble long after schoolroom days were done. She has great gifts, and genius must always be a little uncomfortable at court. She could have made a name for herself as an artist, a singer, a dancer.

Like all young girls, she went through a phase when she could be extremely tiresome. She would dawdle over her dressing, pleased to know she kept us waiting. I cured her of this foible by going off with Lilibet and the pony and leaving her behind.

Sometimes in the evening we had cinema shows in the schoolroom. There was a man in the village who had a movie projector and a lot of old films of Charlie Chaplin and Laurel and Hardy. Sir Basil Brooke and I got hold of him and arranged for an occasional evening's show. All the staff came, and anyone else who cared to.

At the end of these performances we frequently had another, when Alah would try to get Margaret to bed. Margaret would bounce on the sofa, and dodge Alah round chairs, while I talked to the guests, watching all this out of a corner of my eye. When the business looked like getting out of hand I would fix Margaret with a certain stony look, take her arm and walk her to the door, saying, *'Go to bed!'* Margaret usually went then, quietly.

Under all her pranks and tricks she had the softest heart. It was to be her misfortune that the ordinary exploits of adolescence, the natural life of a healthy and vivacious girl, in her case made newspaper paragraphs, instead of being dismissed with a laugh.

One of the people who came up to stay at that time was Sir Richard Molyneux. He is one of the four or five people still living who took part in the famous charge at Omdurman, in the Sudan campaign. Mr Churchill is one of the others. The children were never tired of hearing how, when Sir Richard was wounded, a piece of skin was taken from Mr Churchill's thigh and grafted on to Sir Richard's hand. He used to show it to them both with considerable pride.

Christmas drew nearer, that first Christmas of the war none of us will ever forget. There was still no definite news of what was to happen to us, and whether the children would be allowed to go south or not. If they remained in Scotland, I knew I must give up any hopes of spending Christmas at my own home.

Then, on 18 December, the telephone rang. I picked up the receiver, and my heart gave a great thump, for I heard the

Queen's voice. It sounded, in that moment, quite bright and gay and young again.

'Crawfie! All's well. We're going to spend Christmas at Sandringham as usual.'

There were shouts of joy from the children.

'And you,' the Queen continued, 'can go home, and join us later.'

There were shouts of joy from Crawfie!

Then we all kissed very fondly and they said, 'You will come. You will come, won't you, as soon as Mummie wants you?'

The Royal Family went to Sandringham and had as happy a Christmas there as they could have. This was during the period of the 'phoney war' when nothing was happening. They stayed at Sandringham until 2 February, which was rather longer than usual, with the King and Queen coming down to London, the children remaining there.

Having Christmas at Sandringham was a piece of courage that has been overlooked, for Sandringham is on the east coast, very handy for German bombs. To date none had fallen, but there was no guarantee they would not come. After the collapse of Poland the phoney war was in full swing, but all the air was full of an unpleasant sensation of waiting for worse to come.

The Christmas routine at Sandringham was the same year after year. The children would have resented any change in it, as of old they had objected to my altering a word of a familiar and loved story. The Christmas tree was always lit on Christmas Eve – a custom which I believe came from Germany – Christmas dinner being the high spot of Christmas Day.

Everyone had his own table with his presents laid out. The housekeeper had found out beforehand what the maids hoped for, the steward had done the same for the menservants. The King and Queen shook hands with every member of their staff after the present-giving. Before the war, the household got whatever they had wished for.

The Christmas of 1939 was to be the last of the familiar Christmases for some time, but no one knew it then.

'Perhaps we were too happy,' Lilibet wrote me in one of her letters, and afterwards, when we were all together again, she said wistfully, 'I kept thinking of those sailors, Crawfie, and what Christmas must have been like in their homes.'

Then I got a wire from the Queen, 'Please come to Royal Lodge. Can you come on the fifth?' I went to Royal Lodge and found the children there, and we remained until 12 May, 1940.

Between February and May at Royal Lodge we had a really happy time. You couldn't be anything else but fairly happy there. There weren't the anxious faces one would see in London.

The Queen never showed that she was worried. At that time she seemed to drop her cares at the gates of Royal Lodge and became just Mummie during her stay there. We discussed the war and what would be coming in the future. Many other children from among their own friends were being sent away to safety, but there was no talk of the Princesses going. Later on it was discussed in some of the papers, and I believe some of the ministers were in favour of it, but the idea was turned down.

'The children could not go without me,' the Queen said simply, 'and I could not possibly leave the King.'

We joined up again with the Girl Guide company and got the village children and the evacuees to join up too. In the village school there were about thirty evacuee children from the East End of London. We all became very good friends, and like most real Cockneys, these East End children were easy to get on with and made nothing at all of their suddenly changed surroundings. But I think what they loved most was the delicious meals we provided for them at picnics, and they enjoyed the long hikes with us in the woods.

At weekends, when the King and Queen came down to Royal Lodge, messengers would arrive at all hours with tidings, usually bad. I remember once later on when we were all at Windsor Castle and a long black car hurtled into the courtyard below, undoubtedly bringing a load of trouble, Margaret looked down from the ramparts we were standing on and remarked:

'Boiling lead was a pretty good idea.'

We were leaning over the wall where once guards are said to have poured this down on invaders.

At Royal Lodge we got the schoolroom routine going once again. There were numerous other children staying in and around Windsor, and I got a dancing class up for all of them, which was held once a week. We kept it for little girls only. The Princesses did not understand the antics of little boys, and this did not seem to be the moment to teach them. Miss Vacani, a famous London dancing mistress, used to come out to us there. The little girls came with their nannies, wearing their party frocks, and afterwards we gave them tea. It made a bright break in those gloomy war days.

Lilibet resumed her lessons with Sir Henry Marten at Eton College. As we came and went through the crowded quadrangle I often wondered sadly how many of the boys we saw there would come through the war years. A great many of them never did.

CHAPTER VII

'A House in the Country'

I N London the King and Queen led a busy and wearing life. The King was incessantly in touch with his ministers, the Queen encouraged the various war efforts and organizations and visited the bombed areas. Her gentle sympathy must have been a great comfort to many poor people in those days.

There was one point in the war when different kings and queens were arriving at Buckingham Palace, and the place was full of them. One day Queen Wilhelmina arrived with nothing but the clothes she stood up in. There was a great deal of hasty shopping to be done, and the Queen instructed her own dressmakers to call upon the Dutch Queen, who needed a hat.

Large boxes full of hats were sent round for her to choose from, but none of them appealed at all to Her Majesty. At last she looked up at the middle-aged woman dressed in neat black who had come along to carry the boxes and was wearing a sensible black hat with a brim.

'There you are. That', said Queen Wilhelmina firmly, 'is the hat for me!'

The whole Palace was on edge in those days. There was incessant activity of people arriving and people going, not knowing where they were going to, or whether they would come back again, or whether they would retain their thrones. All who came were made welcome by the King and Queen, who threw their homes open to them for as long as they cared to stay, just as other folks took in their stranded neighbours.

Sometimes during the weekend the Queen would come to my room when the children were in bed and talk to me very anxiously, as any mother might at such a time. Her Majesty had the same conviction as I and so many other women I spoke to. We knew in our hearts we would come through, however hard and bitter the way. We knew in our hearts no invasion would take place. It was a case of woman's intuition, but once again it was proved right.

I remember how one night she paused in the doorway as she left my room and smiled at me. 'We little thought, did we, Crawfie, all we would have to go through,' she said.

Everyone on the estate had evacuee children living with them, mostly from the East End of London. Many of them joined our Guide company, and the little Princesses took a great interest in them all, soon got to know their names, and now the old cry of 'Wait for me, Lilibet' echoed round once more in all sorts of accents, Cockney predominating.

From time to time these same children, now grown up, cross the Princesses' paths, and it is always an immense pleasure to them to find they are remembered, often in spite of considerable changes in shape and size. On her way to Italy, Margaret paused on her journey through the airport to say, 'Hello, Jo. Fancy seeing you here!' to a pretty air hostess who had been one of our Guide company. She remembered the Princess well enough, but probably never expected the Princess would remember her.

It was amusing and no doubt very instructive for the two Princesses to mingle with the children there, for if among the children of court and other officials there had been a tendency to let them have an advantage, win a game, or be relieved of the more sordid tasks, there was nothing of the kind now. It was each for herself.

When we went hiking the Princesses found left for them a very fair share indeed of the dirty work, like gathering firewood and scavenging up. When we camped out in the grounds of Windsor Castle I remember seeing Lilibet standing and looking ruefully at a large cauldron full of greasy dishes into which she had to plunge her arms and do the washing-up.

They were always extremely good about anything like this, and never in all my time with them did I come across any malingering or efforts to bilk unpleasant jobs. They were more than willing to pull their weight.

We had all the business of ration books and clothing coupons to cope with. Alah let out tucks and put in pleats in great feats of mend and make-do. The whole family had this problem. The Queen and Queen Mary were given a certain number over and above the ordinary ration for their official clothes and garments for State occasions. The children had the ordinary allowance, and no more.

I remember more than once the Queen would stop and say, 'There is the very scarf I want!' only to be advised by her dresser that the royal coupons were already extremely low.

No one minded all this as much as Alah, who would willingly have gone without anything herself, but felt her Princesses ought to have everything they wanted. The children had already a good store of both winter and summer frocks and suits, and the Queen had done much generous buying at the British Industries and other fairs and bazaars so that there was a large stock of cottons and tweeds on hand.

Sir Ulick Alexander, Keeper of the Privy Purse, who pays all the Palace expenses and manages the King's private income, had a supply for footmen's uniforms and housemaids' dresses, and linen replacements. But he, too, had to be very careful.

Later the King very wisely put all the men staff at the

Palace and Windsor Castle into navy-blue battle-dress, with 'G. R. VI' embroidered on the breast pocket. This was both comfortable and smart. It also did away with the sore problem of laundry, which in those days was one of life's large-sized worries and hit the Palace as much as the ordinary housewife.

The Palace washing was sent out to a London laundry which, like all others, was short of staff, transport, and soap. Sheets and pillow-cases, collars and shirts would often be absent from home not the usual week, but a month or even six weeks.

On 12 May, the Queen, who was in London with the King, rang me up at eleven o'clock to say, 'Crawfie, I think you had better go at once to Windsor Castle, anyway for the rest of the week.' I warned the footmen and Ainslie, and said we had to pack. I had a feeling in my bones when packing that it would be much longer than just a weekend, so I packed all my belongings and all my books which I wanted. Then the children arrived at four, and I told them the news.

At seven o'clock that night we drove down the Long Walk to Windsor Castle. Alah had taken only clothes for the weekend for the Princesses and herself, and she had to return to Royal Lodge for the rest. I was the only one who did not have to go back later and repack. We remained at Windsor Castle for five years, until the war ended.

In the gathering twilight of that May evening I saw the great bulk rising out of the shadows as I had seen it on another evening many years before as I came south. Like a fortress in a fairy-story. But now we all knew who the ogre was!

A small paragraph appeared in the English and American papers. It said the Royal children had been evacuated to 'a house in the country'.

Windsor Castle was a fortress, not a home, and we were always very much aware of this. It is replete with every kind of historical trophy. There is the shirt that Charles I was executed in, and the bullet that came out of Nelson's heart, and Bonnie Prince Charlie's sword as well as King Henry VIII's armour.

It would take years to tell of all the extraordinary things that are preserved there. Though interesting, I personally found them somewhat sinister things to share a shelter with.

It was beginning to get dark when we arrived. We were tired, and it was very gloomy. Pictures had been removed, and all the beautiful glass chandeliers had been taken down. The State Apartments were muffled in dust-sheets, their glass-fronted cupboards turned to the walls. About the stone passages the shadowy figures of servants and firemen loomed, attending to the blackout. I remember one old man remarking to me dryly:

'By the time we've blacked out all the windows here, it's morning again, miss.'

The two little girls clung to me apprehensively. Alah, as always when she was bothered or anxious, was cross. We none of us quite knew what was going to happen, and Alah and I, at any rate, knew very well that the war was going to enter into a much more definite stage, and that the King and Queen in London were probably in considerable danger.

All night long ghostly figures flitted around, their feet echoing in the stone passages – ARP wardens watching for beams and chinks of light showing through the blackout. We tried our best to laugh it all off, but that first night most of us had a shiver down our spines and the feeling that the war had caught up with us.

The children had their usual quarters in the Lancaster Tower, where they had always stayed when they came with their parents to Windsor. The court had always gone there for Easter and Lilibet's birthday. The Lancaster Tower is three storeys high, and dates from Henry VII's time. Lilibet had her own bedroom and a bathroom, sharing the former with Bobo, an arrangement I was glad of at this juncture. For Bobo is a sensible Scottish lass, who one felt would come calm and unperturbed through innumerable bombardments. She hails from a place in Inverness-shire called the Black Isle.

Margaret and Alah had rooms next door. The nursery was adjoining. This was an ordinary sitting room adapted for the children with toy-cupboards. It looks over Windsor Park. Bathrooms had been let into the tremendously thick walls of the Castle, bringing the place more up to date. But there is no central heating of any kind there. There are electric stoves in the bedrooms, which were considerably affected, as everywhere else, by fuel cuts, and had a way of going out altogether at the coldest moments. There were log fires in the sitting rooms. To travel the icy passages from sitting room up to bed was a feat of considerable endurance. I often wore fur boots under my evening dress.

I was all on my own, quite a way from anyone else, in the Victoria Tower. It was approached by the usual winding staircase. I had a large bedroom and sitting room, but my bathroom was out on the roof. This was a chilly arrangement, and when the bombs began to fall, not too comfortable. I always hoped that, if one had to come that way, it would choose a convenient moment!

The warning arrangements had been carefully thought out and organized before we arrived, and a system of bells had been installed which were operated by the wardens, who knew what was happening, and were in communication by telephone with the watchers on the roofs. There was a special bell which rang when we had to go down to the shelter.

We all felt lost at first. The nights were so dark and we did not know what was happening. The children were cross, too, because so many of the things they wanted were still at Royal Lodge.

Lord Wigram was Governor of the Castle. He was very bothered and worried at this new responsibility that had come to him. I had nothing to do with the children after six o'clock, and it was arranged that Alah would bring them down to the shelter when there was a red warning. This meant aircraft were directly overhead.

At the end of our first talk at Windsor I remember feeling rather amused, because the Master of the Household, who was then Sir Hill Child, told me dinner would be at eight in the Octagon Room. 'We dress,' he said gravely.

The Octagon Room was an oak-panelled apartment a long walk from my rooms in the Victoria Tower. I did not know my way, and there were hardly any lights. At ten to eight I started down the stairs to try to find the dining room, which seems easy now, but there was no one to ask and nobody to direct me, and for some time I wandered around like one of the Castle's ghosts. I was wearing a red velvet dinner-dress against the Britannic draughts that raged through the stone passages. I found the gentlemen on my arrival all convention-ally attired in dinner-jackets with black ties.

Household dinner was pretty grim. Sir Gerald Kelly was staying at the Castle at work on the Coronation portraits. There were also Sir Hill Child, Sir Dudley Colles, and myself. We were an ill-assorted party, and all of us were anxious and a little depressed anyway. To make matters worse, the light was very poor. All the glass chandeliers had been taken down because they would make splinters, and all the high-powered bulbs had been taken out by the ARP and low-powered ones substituted. We seemed to live in sort of underworld.

New blood seemed essential if we were all to remain friends. So I decided to get Monty, Mrs Montaudon-Smith, to come back and help me, among other things, with the lessons.

I was able to do this only after some persuasion. Monty liked a Bohemian life and was all against being beleaguered for any length of time in a fortress. But in the end she did come, and she brightened things up a lot. The children were very fond of her, and they loved singing with her.

We were all ensconced in the Castle, with Alah in the nursery, at the time the first bombs fell on Windsor. About two nights after we were settled in, the alarm bell went. I had bought a siren suit which was very like Mr Churchill's, only it was made of green velvet. I was rather pleased to put it on. It had been arranged that I would not collect the children and Alah, because that might have been difficult since I was a long way off; and in any case, Alah was responsible for seeing they got to the shelter.

I had taken on the post of helping in the Red Cross centre there. I kept the keys and was responsible for the cupboards of the medicine- and dressing-chests. Everyone was doing a job of some sort like that.

At the sound of the alarm bell I went at once to the shelter. There was no sign of the children and no sign of Alah, and everyone was in a state of fuss. Sir Hill Child came and said, 'This is impossible. They simply must come.'

I ran all the way to the nurseries, where I could hear a great deal of commotion going on. I shouted, 'Alah!'

Very often she thought my voice was the Queen's, and she would say, 'Yes, Your Majesty,' and would be absolutely furious afterwards over her error. I said, 'It's not Your Majesty, Alah, it's Crawfie. Lord Wigram and Sir Hill Child and everybody else is waiting in the shelter and you must come down. This is not a dress rehearsal. What are you doing?'

Alah was always very careful. Her cap had to be put on, and her white uniform.

Lilibet called, 'We're dressing, Crawfie. We must dress.'

I said, 'Nonsense! You are not to dress. Put a coat over your night clothes, at once.'

They finally came to the shelter. By this time Sir Hill Child was a nervous wreck. He stood rather in awe of Alah, but he said, 'You must understand the Princesses must come down at once. They must come down whatever they are wearing.'

The shelter was in one of the dungeons, not a particularly inviting place anyway. There lingered about it always the memory of others who had probably been incarcerated there, and left some of their unhappiness behind them. The atmosphere was gloomy, and there were beetles. The walls had all been reinforced, and beds put up, but that first night for some reason nothing was ready. Later on the shelters were made quite comfortable, with a bedroom for the King and Queen and the Princesses, and proper bathroom arrangements, but just at the start there was a good bit of improvisation.

The little girls were very good. They took it all most calmly. Margaret fell asleep on my knee. Lilibet lay down and read a book. Someone came along presently and whispered to me that there was a red warning. I sat nursing Margaret, straining my ears, and praying for the night to pass.

It was two in the morning before the all-clear sounded. Towards the end of our vigil Sir Hill Child made tea. He is a tall, distinguished-looking person, very dignified, and even in this crisis he managed to look spruce and well dressed, with a scarf round his neck. There was something incongruous in his meticulous tinkerings with the teacups as he waited for the kettle to boil. I thought how little I had dreamed, as a girl in Scotland, that the time would come when I would drink tea in a royal dungeon at midnight, with German bombers droning overhead.

At two o'clock Sir Hill Child bowed ceremoniously to Lilibet. 'You may now go to bed, ma'am,' he said.

They trooped rather wearily up and we had peace the rest of that night.

In the morning I had a talk with Lilibet, who could always see the sense of things. She quite realized that proper beds would have to be put down in the dungeon, and blankets and their treasures would also be put there so they would not have to go and collect them. I had them each get their little suitcases. The French nation once gave them a set of beautiful dolls, and these dolls had all the jewel cases and things that ladies have. One was pink and the other blue. The children packed the cases that morning with their favourite brooches, the things that they wear every day which did not need to go into the safe. They had books, and each had a little diary with a lock which they always wrote up every night. That was something on which the Queen had insisted; as soon as they could write she gave them these beautiful locking diaries which they religiously filled in each night before they fell asleep.

After that the children got proper siren suits. When the bombing got really bad we all slept downstairs in the dungeon. You could see the Princesses going off at seven with their little cases as if they were going to catch a train at Paddington, wearing their siren suits.

We sometimes had warnings in the daytime, and if we happened to be outside we sheltered in various summerhouses. King George III had built some curious caves in the side of a hill quite close to the Castle. They were entered by a long tunnel which leads to a vast cave, the wall studded with pebbles. They smell very damp and horrid. Margaret loved to run on ahead and jump out at us, shouting 'Boo!' when we took cover there from daytime bombs. Later the house staff did their gas tests in there, so the caves probably for the first time were of some real use.

A company of Grenadier Guards came three days after we arrived. We were introduced to Sir Francis Manners and four officers who lived in the Castle and came to meals. I thought this was wonderful. Lilibet was now fourteen, growing up, and it gave an opportunity to teach her to play hostess. I planned to have parties, too, and I felt we could keep things cheerful for the children.

The officers were charming. They came to household breakfast. We had very gay lunch parties with the children, Lilibet and Margaret and Sir Dudley Colles, Sir Gerald Kelly and three officers. The officers loved to meet the two girls and talk to them. Lunch was quite a long meal which started at perhaps quarter to one and went on until three.

Lilibet played the part of hostess perfectly. She never left anybody hanging around. She chose who would sit on *her* right and who on *her* left. Margaret always sat opposite her sister and chose who would sit on her right and on her left. It was pleasant to see these children getting their party seated in a very short time. Lilibet had seen her father as host many times, of course, and in addition I made her pour tea for us at Birkhall. Children should learn to do these things young. Lilibet had very natural good manners and was an excellent conversationalist.

Margaret began to develop into a real personality then with the male element about. She kept everyone in fits of laughter, and she had a gay little way with her that won everybody's heart in that gloomy old Castle.

The officers dug slit trenches all over the grounds, and the children had names for them – Denny's Delight, and Peter's Folly – after the officers who dug them. These trenches were more of a menace to us than anything else; you did not know when you would trip over one while on a walk through the grounds.

Presently the officers asked us to tea in the guardroom. It was a special tea party got up for the little girls. The batman had obviously borrowed one of the best tablecloths from the housekeeper, and some cups, and a great deal of trouble had been taken to give the children a good tea. There was a large bowl of cherries, chocolate cakes, and a wonderful assortment of little cakes, which they had had mostly sent from their homes.

Everybody was very gay, and Lilibet was pleased because she was asked to be hostess and pour tea. The children were also greatly delighted when they were asked to add their names to the numerous signatures on the plastered walls. There were some rather skittish paintings that had been done by soldiers past and present, but we tactfully ignored these.

After tea we played guessing games and charades, and I think the officers were as sorry as we were when the party was over. These young men were all far away from homes where they must have had sisters, and I am sure it must have given them just for a little while a feeling of home.

Windsor Castle was a wonderful place on wet days. There was so much of it to be explored, so many odd nooks and cor-ners where we had never been before. One day the King's Librarian, Sir Owen Morshead, took us right down to the vaults under the Castle.

'Would you like to see something interesting?' he asked us. We said we would. He showed us a lot of rather ordinary-looking leather hatboxes which seemed at first sight just to be all stuffed up with old newspapers. But when we examined these, we discovered the Crown Jewels were hidden in them!

We saw little of Queen Mary during the war. She joined the Duke and Duchess of Beaufort in their country house in Gloucestershire. This she had been most loath to do. If she could have had her own way she would have sat out the war firmly in London. But she was an old lady already, and I think in the end the King persuaded her it would save them all anxiety to know she was safe.

There was nobody in the whole of England who went in for austerity to such a degree as Queen Mary. She kept everybody busy from morning till night with knitting-parties, or rolling bandages, and she in person would go out into the woods and assist with the felling of trees.

The house was large and damp, but nothing would induce Her Majesty to take any advantages or to have more than her rightful share of the scarce fuel. The central heating was cut off, and Her Majesty insisted they live on their rations only. Her household suffered accordingly.

During the war years, when possible, the King and Queen paid regular weekend visits to Windsor Castle, arriving on Fridays in time for tea at five o'clock. Very often the Princesses and I would take Jock on a rein and Hans, the Norwegian pony, and three dogs – Crackers, Susan, and Ching – along an avenue leading to one of the main gates to meet Mummie and Papa.

There was great excitement when the two cars appeared in the distance, the leading one with the King and Queen and Mr Cameron, the King's detective, beside the chauffeur; the second with the equerry and lady-in-waiting. We all started to run towards them – horses, dogs, and ourselves – and the car slowed down to a crawl and stopped. I remember how tired the King and Queen looked, and how very happy and relieved they were to see their daughters so cheerful and leading a comparatively natural life in spite of the war.

If by chance the cars were late or came by a different avenue, we kept our eye on the Round Tower where the King's standard was hoisted by an old retired sailor. When we saw the standard we got back as quickly as we could to the Castle. I often used to wonder how our old navy man timed the hoisting so beautifully. I found out that the ritual at Buckingham Palace, Windsor Castle, or Royal Lodge is the same: whenever the King leaves Buckingham Palace a message is sent by telephone to the Castle or to Royal Lodge, the journey takes roughly an hour, the old man at Windsor climbs to his perch, and from his eyrie sees the car far away on the road. At the moment of its entering the Castle, up goes the standard.

After that the Castle becomes alive with activity. His Majesty is in residence. Everyone is on the alert.

Later the luggage brake comes along with the Queen's dresser and the King's valet, plus piles of luggage.

Jane for many years was a great favourite of Princess Elizabeth's. She was one of the corgis and the mother of Crackers and Carol, born on Christmas Day at Sandringham – hence the names.

Jane was out with us one afternoon and as usual was rabbiting madly. Unfortunately she dashed after her prey across one of the drives and was run over by one of the gardeners at Windsor. He, poor man, was shaken and very upset, because he knew how devoted the Princess was to Jane. Princess Elizabeth was very sad but assured him again and again that it was no fault of his, and that she should have taken greater care of the dog.

When we returned Princess Elizabeth sat down at once and wrote a most charming note to the gardener. She was always a very kind-hearted little girl.

Princess Elizabeth gave her first broadcast to the children of England in those distressing days of 1940 when families were being torn apart and every village and country town was full of poor, homesick little scraps longing for Mummie. Both Lilibet and Margaret, being themselves evacuated to 'a house in the country', knew something of the general break-up of familiar home life, and it was decided that Lilibet should speak to other children herself.

She was so good about the endless rehearsals we had to have to get the breathing and phrasing right. It was a long and tedious business for a little girl. She read her speech several times to Mummie and Papa. Though royal speeches in general are more or less mapped out beforehand from a policy point of view, a great deal is put in by the family themselves, and the Queen especially has that rather sweet human touch which is so helpful in making these occasions sound intimate rather than purely official.

Lilibet herself put in several phrases that were quite her own, and everyone who heard this particular speech will remember the most spontaneous and amusing end. Lilibet, always anxious to bring her small sister forward, said, 'Come, Margaret, say good night,' and a small, clear voice piped in rather pompously, 'Good night, children.'

A BBC official came down to superintend the broadcast. From the letters that came in afterwards, it was plain that a great many grown-ups as well as children had listened in, and found the experience a very touching one.

Lilibet was always too serious-minded to play practical jokes and never failed to consider what the feelings of the people would be if anything of this sort were to be played on them. Perhaps she longed to do it at moments, but Margaret and I always had to urge her to do anything mischievous, like removing the broom from the gardener's barrow at Windsor Castle and hiding it among the bushes.

Margaret and I were very given to practical jokes, and we each egged the other on to play them. We would laugh to see the man looking vaguely around, wondering what on earth had happened, then look in astonishment into the barrow. We then became rather ashamed, and I would say, 'We really must go and show him where it is,' but Margaret would say, 'We can't. He must find it.'

I think that particular old gardener got to know our habits and kept a very keen eye open. If anything disappeared he knew he had only to look around the nearest bush to find it.

Lilibet was always ashamed of us on these occasions and walked away from us rather pink in the face. She laughed to see what was going on, but did not want to be party to anything of the sort in any way.

At Windsor Castle during the war we always longed to ring the alarm bell on the terrace. It was supposed to be rung only by the sergeant. When the bell was rung it brought out the whole guard all over the Castle. Margaret and I put Lilibet into a frenzy of nerves by opening the door to the little box. We would touch the bell but not press it, whereupon she would rush into the Castle with the dogs and say, 'You can't do it. You can't do it!'

However, Margaret and I never had the nerve really to bring out the whole guard; that would have been something with which the King would have had to deal.

One day the Major in command, who had, I think, seen us doing this and knew what we wanted to do, said to us, 'You may, if you like, ring it any morning you like this week, just off-hand. You can do it, because this is the week for practising the bringing out of the guard to see how quickly they can assemble.'

I said to Margaret, 'This is your chance. Go down before breakfast and just ring the bell.'

But she got into a state of giggles and nerves and said, 'Oh, I couldn't possibly.'

I said, 'You've been longing to do it for months, you know.'

She said, 'No, Crawfie, you do it,' and now I could not get either of them to go, although we had been given permission to ring it.

I usually went to breakfast at nine, and one day I went down early, at eight-thirty. Two faces appeared at a bedroom window where they had been waiting for ages to see me go down the steps.

I looked up and said, 'I'm going to do it!'

Their faces went pink. 'Oh, do hurry! The sentry is coming round the corner. Hurry up, Crawfie! Hurry up!'

Then I was beginning to be nervous myself, because I thought, *Dear me, I have only got to put my finger on this bell and the whole guard of the Castle will drop what they are doing and run. It's much too much. Even I can't do it.*

I looked up and said, 'I can't do it.'

And they said, 'Oh, you're a coward. Go on!'

I opened the door and pressed the bell. Immediately I heard bells tingling all over the Castle, down the slopes, down the drive. Every bell in England seemed to be ringing.

The Princesses tried not to go into shrieks of laughter. They said my face was a complete picture of horror at what I had done, and I speedily went through to breakfast rather red in the face. I met some of the officers who had been in the middle of their breakfast, running along the corridor.

I managed to ask, 'What's wrong? Is there a fire alarm?'

And one said, 'Oh, no, the usual routine bell for parade, but we have not had one for days, and perhaps there is something wrong. We're going to find out.'

There was one wonderful night at Windsor when there was a scare of parachutists arriving, and every precaution was taken. The guardsmen were ready with tommy-guns. We had two cream-coloured Norwegian ponies in one of the fields who were just foals and quite young. At about midnight I heard a great commotion in the grounds of the Castle, and couldn't think what it could be. I looked out of the window. In the distance on the grass I saw two little white figures flitting about. The soldiers were running, but luckily they did not shoot, for it was discovered that in the thunderstorm which had just ended the foals had got very frightened, jumped the fences and raced all over the grounds, with half the trained company of Grenadier Guards after them. After this wonderful midnight chase for parachutists, they found only two very frightened little foals down near the river.

At Windsor during the war we were given our helmets and gas masks and were also given an intriguing little box marked Iron Rations, which we kept close to our helmets in a hold-all. We also had plugs for our ears to be used when the guns went off. Princess Elizabeth used to set us a great example by wearing her gas mask every day as required, and by carefully cleaning the eyepiece every evening with the ointment provided.

The gas chamber was brought to Windsor to test the masks. I went through it; the children did not, for I felt that was unnecessary. Stupidly enough, I came up from it and stood in front of the fire, and all the gas regenerated again off my tweeds and nearly killed me.

The long slow months went by, and we remained incarcerated and cut off in Windsor Castle. They were monotonous days, but certain incidents stand out. All through one lovely early-summer day we could hear the sound of far-off shattering explosions and gunfire. Aircraft kept coming over. The little girls were bothered and anxious about their father and mother, and kept pausing in their play to ask anxiously:

'Crawfie, whatever is it?'

I was at least able to assure them that whatever was taking place, it was not in London. I knew it was too far off for that; and I was right. It was at Dunkirk, where the army was being taken off the beaches by the little boats. We had all seen an Admiralty notice in the papers, asking would anyone owning a small boat of any kind take or send it to a rendezvous, but no one knew exactly what it was for. So the news given out over the wireless came as a shock, mixed with thankfulness that most of our men had escaped. There had been vague rumours that the army was cut off, but most of them came from abroad, and no one knew what to believe.

We kept a large map with flags on it which we moved from place to place, and I kept the little girls up to date as far as possible with what was happening.

It was with profound relief, I remember, that they both rushed to speak to their parents on the telephone that evening, and learned that they were still quite all right.

Lilibet developed rapidly, and those quiet months at Windsor helped a lot. For the first time she was on her own, away from her parents. At various mealtimes and when we gave parties, it was she who had to do the honours, play hostess, and see to the seating of her guests. She who had been a rather shy little girl became a very charming young person, able to cope with any situation without awkwardness.

We had lunch all together with the household, and school-room tea, but they still kept up the old habit of a simple nursery dinner.

CHAPTER VIII

Gas Masks and Pantomimes

THE King and Queen remained at Buckingham Palace all through the London blitz. There were times when we felt extremely anxious about them. Ineffective efforts were made in official circles to get them to go away to a safer place. Accommodation had been arranged for them secretly that would not be so simple a landmark for the enemy as Buckingham Palace was, or even Windsor Castle which, being on the Thames, was rather easy to locate from the air.

There were evenings in that summer of 1941 when London was under fire, when we all felt anxious. Windsor is near enough to London for what was going on there to be only too evident to us all. The Castle is built on chalk, and vibrations were felt from great distances.

To divert the little girls' attention, we would play the piano, and they would sing their duets at the top of their voices. When I think back on it now, there was through all this an immense amount of laughter and fun in spite of it all, so that sometimes Lilibet, who was a very thoughtful little girl, would pause and say:

'Oh, Crawfie, *do* you think we are being too happy?'

I replied, 'Mummie and Papa want you to be happy, and we shall not help anything or anyone if we sit in corners and cry, shall we?'

The little girls lived for Friday nights, when their parents would come if it was at all possible. It was heartbreaking to see how all this was telling on Their Majesties. The Queen's charming and youthful face became pale and drawn, and the great strain she was undergoing showed in her eyes. The King came suddenly to look very much like his father.

But the royal discretion still held. Unpleasant or bothersome matters were never discussed. When they came down to Windsor we took up the pleasant family life again for a little while, and tried to live those three short days as if there were nothing else.

Then came Monday, or often even Sunday night, and they had to go.

Food grew scarce. Now we all looked forward greedily to our Sunday-morning egg, the only one we got. We had it fried until fat became scarce.

Ration books and gas masks we all had had for some time. It had been difficult to fit the little girls properly. After several abortive efforts they were issued Mickey Mouse masks, horrible affairs with red-and-blue noses that put us in mind of the mandrill at the Zoo.

We had to put on these contraptions every day and wear them for ten minutes to get used to them. We made a game of it, wore them out-of-doors, and played in the woods at being prehistoric monsters, which I am sure we closely resembled. When the children got over their first qualms it all became funny and we laughed a lot, which resulted in some very curious noises emerging. Gas masks are not intended for laughing in.

One day as we were doing our daily ten minutes we saw a mysterious figure skulking from tree to tree in a most suspicious manner, obviously trying to get away without being seen.

A spy! we thought. Forgetting we still wore our gas masks, we followed him through the woods, but presently lost him. Our last view of him was running wildly through the thicket.

We hurried back to the Castle. The warning was sounded and the police turned out. Presently a terrified plumber boy was rounded up. He had liked the look of us all in our gas masks much less than we liked the look of him.

We knitted, Lilibet making manful efforts to improve her skill. Margaret and I collected acorns and beech huskings, painted them in gay colours and made them into ornaments to be worn in buttonholes. We sold these for the war effort and made five pounds.

We were still at Windsor when Christmas came round again. It did not look like being a very merry one for anybody. So I decided we would do a Christmas play, *The Christmas Child*, we had rehearsed but had never performed at Birkhall. This proved to be a great diversion for everyone.

We gave the show in St George's Hall at the Castle. The altar there is not consecrated, so we were able to have the play round it. Windsor Castle is a wonderful place for anything of this kind, there were so many pieces of brocade and tapestry and suitable oddments we could borrow for dressing up.

Lilibet had a golden crown and a velvet tunic, and she was one of the Kings. The Black King was one of the evacuees, a boy whom we blackened with cocoa, and the other King was also an evacuee.

We had the Little Child in the shepherd's hut, and that was Margaret. It was a simple scene with a rocking cradle. She wore a little white dress and a string of turquoise beads, and she sang 'Gentle Jesus, Meek and Mild'. I can still see that little figure and the cradle. She had a most beautifully clear voice and she sang it all alone, with that great hall half-full of people.

Unfortunately, I could not see what was happening when the play was actually given. We were behind two double doors at the back so that we never saw the play in full production. We ushered the children through and had them so well trained that they did the whole thing.

All who took part walked through the audience, Lilibet leading, carrying the frankincense and myrrh. The shepherds were all schoolboys. They had scarves around their heads and very much looked the part, and did a very good murmuring scene.

The King and Queen were absolutely amazed at the entire performance, and so was everybody else. That was the beginning of the children's acting. The money we got from that quite overwhelmed us. We felt we could not ask for money for the seats, but we passed a collection plate and got about thirty pounds.

The success of our first effort made us ambitious. One day I said half jokingly, 'I really believe we could do a pantomime.' From that moment I had no peace. Margaret was after me incessantly. 'Crawfie, you *did* say ... ' she would begin a dozen times a week. She produced drawings of Aladdin. She arranged all the parts. She talked pantomime constantly, and it was a great deal to do with her persistence that in the end we began to think very seriously about it. Margaret knows what she wants, and she never lets go.

I spoke to the King about it one weekend. He said rather absently, obviously ready to do anything that would keep the children's minds busy and give them a little fun, 'By all means have a pantomime, Crawfie, if you think it a good idea.' I don't think for a moment he took the matter seriously.

There was a schoolmaster at the Royal School at Windsor Great Park named Hubert Tanner. The school was built by Queen Victoria for the estate children. The schoolmaster was a delightful Welshman who at one time, I knew, had been a

The Girl Guide Princesses. Princess Elizabeth fixes a large arm-sling on her sister during first-aid practice

During an evening together round the fire, the King reads a book while the Queen helps Princess Elizabeth with her knitting

Princess Elizabeth gives her attention to a knotty problem

*From their allotments at Windsor Castle, diligently worked by themselves,
the Princesses gather a fine harvest of dwarf beans*

Sixteen-year-old Princess Elizabeth registers at the Windsor Office of the Ministry of Labour under the youth registration scheme started during the war

Windsor Castle, seen from the air

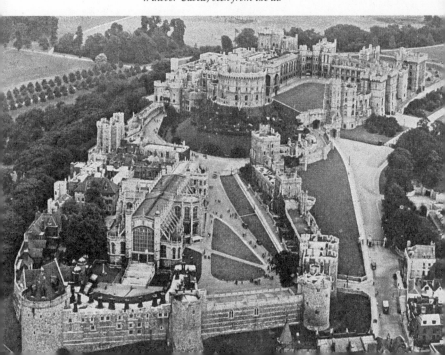

The Princesses emerge as competent actresses in their first pantomime – Cinderella

In her ball-dress, Princess Margaret sits with the Queen while 'Principal Boy' Elizabeth rehearses her part

The Royal Family at stirrup-pump practice. Princess Elizabeth struggles with a recalcitrant nozzle

Princess Elizabeth photographed with one of the farm horses during a royal inspection of the harvest at Sandringham

*Princess Elizabeth as Aladdin and Princess Margaret
as Princess Roxana in the 1943 royal pantomime*

The King and Queen spend a quiet evening at the Palace

The Princesses have always been very fond of reading. Here, Princess Elizabeth points out something of interest in her sister's book

Princess Elizabeth makes friends with the ponies at Windsor

Princess Margaret with Sue

*Princess Margaret with Gypsy. She is holding
the cup won by the horse in an
Appearance and General Behaviour
competition at a Windsor show*

*In May 1944, Princess Elizabeth
arrives at the New Theatre to attend her
first opera – the Sadler's Wells
Company in* La Bohème

Prince Philip 'incognito'. He grew the beard while serving with the Pacific Fleet in 1947

Princess Elizabeth in khaki. At the wheel of a ambulance at the ATS Training Centre

The heir presumptive gains first-hand experience of a task all too familiar to most motorists

*On V Day 1945, the Royal Family, accompanied by a jubilant Mr Churchill,
come out on the Palace balcony in response to the chanting of the rejoicing crowds*

A year later. The Royal Family attend the Victory Parade

An informal family group in the grounds of Royal Lodge, Windsor

The two Princesses pose together at the piano in their private apartments at Buckingham Palace

*A photograph taken in 1946 of Princess Elizabeth
in her own sitting room at Buckingham Palace*

*Princess Elizabeth attends to
the business of the day at her
sitting room desk*

Fulfilling one of her first public engagements, Princess Margaret walks by a line of cots at a day nursery in Bethnal Green

A visit to the British Legion Poppy Factory at Richmond

The scene at a royal garden party at Buckingham Palace, July 1947

Arriving at the Queen Elizabeth's Hospital for Children in Hackney, of which she is President, Princess Elizabeth excites the admiration of the small onlookers

Prince Philip

Gilbert and Sullivan actor himself, and knew a lot about stagecraft and producing. We invited him to tea, and he and I and the children talked it all over.

In the end it was decided Mr Tanner would write a pantomime for his own school children, bringing in all the jokes, and we would then fit in bits for the two Princesses. Then he would produce it at the Castle.

It was not long before he brought us the script, which sounded wonderful. We immediately began rehearsals, at which Mr Tanner himself took charge. This brought the two Princesses into touch with many other children, a thing I had always been keen on. The leading man, who played opposite Lilibet, was one Cyril Wood, a delightful boy, and one of Mr Tanner's star pupils. Later he was to enter the Castle on the staff of the Comptroller of Supplies. The two Princesses thoroughly enjoyed all the pantomime stunts, but most of all the scene where they both sat on one end of a bench, while Cyril Wood sat on the other. They then got up, and he fell on the floor. One day, by way of a change, he got up first, and they both collapsed on to the floor, to their intense amusement.

There was never any nonsense at these rehearsals, and Mr Tanner saw to it that they were all children together, and no one was allowed to feel out of things, or shy. He had a great gift for putting young people at their ease. We all enjoyed these rehearsals very much.

Our first pantomime was *Cinderella*. Margaret had long since made up her mind she would be Cinderella. Lilibet was principal boy. Both the children did their parts extremely well, and in the coach scene Margaret was delightful. There was an old sedan chair on which we put wheels. Margaret had a white wig on, and a crinoline dress, with a small patch on her face, and made a lovely picture as she sat looking out of the golden coach. She brought the house down.

We had wonderful choruses with songs, and we trained in

great style. We drilled all those taking part right up to the very last moment.

All this was of course a great help in taking the young people's minds off the war, and bringing them together with others of their own age.

We had the scenery for the pantomime painted by two kind men whose offer to do it for us was most readily accepted. Everything else we did ourselves. We hired the peasant costumes, the Princesses' dresses, and wigs.

There was great argument about the charge we should make for admission. Lilibet said, 'Oh, you can't ask people to pay seven and sixpence, Crawfie. No one will pay that to look at *us*!'

Margaret said, 'Nonsense! They'll pay anything to see us, and it is for the Queen's Wool Fund.'

The Queen also thought seven and sixpence was rather a lot, but she eventually agreed and that is what we charged for the best seats, second-best five shillings, and on down to a shilling. We had programmes printed, and did everything down to the smallest detail in great style.

The mornings of the pantomimes, Margaret was always sick in bed. Alah would say, 'Miss Crawford, Princess Margaret is absolutely pea-green.' I would go along and look at her, and Margaret, absolutely pea-green, would say, 'It's nothing, Crawfie, it's quite all right.'

'I am not worrying about you in the least,' I told her. 'You'll have to be on the stage at two o'clock, but the morning is yours to do what you like with.'

I rather doubted the first time whether she would make it, but she did, though she was in bed until ten minutes before. But once she got up and had her make-up slapped on, she was perfectly all right.

Lilibet took it all much more calmly, though I know she, too, was very excited. She never showed what she was feeling.

They used to say I had the whitest of faces on the morning of the pantomime.

The King, who until the last moment had never taken the pantomime at all seriously, towards the end of the rehearsals began to take an immense interest. He had never thought it possible his children could do anything of that kind, and he was always amazed by it. He went over the whole thing with me meticulously, as if he were arranging a battle campaign.

'Lilibet cannot possibly wear that,' he told me. 'The tunic is too short.'

He was extremely helpful with suggestions over the dresses, and full of constructive criticism over the articulation of the cast.

'I can't hear a word any of them say,' he would complain from the back of the hall.

In one of our later pantomimes he rearranged the final scene completely, and made it a great success. The whole cast had to march to the tune 'Red, White, and Blue Christmas'. Our attempt had been chaotic, for we had six-foot Guardsmen and small children all cluttered up together. We had arranged a scene in which Union Jacks were unfurled on the stage. The way we had it, all the small children were entirely obliterated. The King reorganized it so that the tall Guardsmen stood at the back of the stage and held the flags there.

All this activity was a very good thing for the younger people who could not do anything much for the war effort. From our pantomimes we raised between eight and nine hundred pounds for the Queen's Wool Fund.

We used the stage and beautiful velvet curtains in the Waterloo Room for our pantomimes. Queen Victoria had had the stage put up in other days, for household theatricals. Round this room there had hung for years wonderful oil-paintings of the kings and queens of bygone times. These were all taken out of their frames during the war, and stacked away in safety.

We had had pantomime posters done in vivid colours for our show, and one day Margaret had a bright idea. We put these posters inside the empty frames. The result was quite ludicrous. There was Dick Whittington with his cat gazing down from a frame marked Charles I. Mother Goose appeared as Queen Henrietta Maria, and so on all round the room.

I had wondered if the King would object, and was a little apprehensive about this, but I need not have bothered. Not long afterwards I heard His Majesty showing someone round and pointing them out, saying, 'What do you think of my ancestors?'

About seventy young officers altogether came and went during our time at Windsor. We kept a record of their names. When the war really got bad and they went off, we would hear from time to time that one had been killed. Princess Elizabeth was always the first to write to the mother of the officer and give her a little picture of how much she had appreciated him at Windsor and what they had talked about. That was entirely her own idea.

Many important people came and went. General Montgomery came to Windsor, where he was made a field-marshal during the war.

The two girls were always immensely interested in airmen. The RAF took their fancy, and the men who went up in aircraft alone were their heroes. When an airman was to be decorated by the King there was quite a flutter in the schoolroom. The Princesses always went down to peep through the doors.

American soldiers came a lot to the Castle. The little girls fascinated them, but it became a little difficult, because one and all they opened the conversation in the same way: 'I have a little girl at home just your age.' It got to a pitch when it was difficult for the children to keep their faces straight, but they struggled manfully.

'Crawfie,' whispered Margaret once to me, 'the children there must be in America, all our age. *Billions* of them!'

The Americans collected postcards of the Princesses. One day there was immense excitement because one of them asked me might he send a box of chocolates to Lilibet. To both the children at this time, sweets of any kind, being scarce, were an immense treat, and they counted the days till the parcel duly arrived.

The little girls were a great addition to these mixed parties, for they used to go round and ask what their children's names were, and would generally help to put shy young men at their ease. It was a great relief to many who came to the Castle for the first time, not quite knowing what to expect, usually over-awed and nervous, to be taken in hand by two high-spirited and normal young girls.

The Royal Family's build-up both at home and abroad never seems to me to be a happy one. There is always an effort made to present them as some sort of superhuman creation, above the run of ordinary people. This has a lowering effect on the spirits, especially of foreigners.

How often have I seen Margaret dispel it entirely by slipping her small hand into a large one and saying, 'Come and look at the gardens,' or, 'Have you seen our horses?'

In June 1944 the war took a sudden turn. An entirely new affliction came upon us. One hot Sunday the Royal Family were as usual at church in St George's Hall in Windsor Castle. News came through that the Guards' Chapel in Wellington Barracks, opposite Buckingham Palace, had had a direct hit by a strange new kind of pilotless aircraft. The place had been wrecked, and a great many people killed, including the sister of the Queen's Treasurer.

I had not been to church that day. I had gone out to lunch. I returned to the Castle to find everything in a state of chaos, the King and Queen anxiously awaiting further news. For the one and only time during the whole war, I saw the Queen really shaken. No one quite knew what this new weapon of frightfulness was, or what it could do. Appalling stories began to go round.

ARP officials and war ministers came in for consultations. Vague threats had hung in the air for some time about a new and horrific weapon, and we could only suppose that this was it.

There had been something human about the old bombers. They were guided by living crews, and anyway, we had all grown accustomed to them. One would cock an ear and listen, and even the little girls would know and say either 'Ours' or 'Theirs' as the bombers went over. They knew the name of every English aircraft and had models of most of them.

We actually had our first sight of a V1 when we were cooking sausages with the Girl Guides in Windsor Park. The Guide captain and I heard the thing coming and we made everyone lie down. I lay next to Margaret, and flung myself across her, and we waited and saw the thing go over us. Mercifully it kept on going. It cut out and dropped on the Windsor Race Course several miles ahead, but we were all shaken by the explosion.

At this time I noticed the little girls showed signs of strain. Conversation would break off and I would know they were listening. Though there was admittedly something oddly fiendish about these things – they were so utterly inhuman, like being chased by a robot – it was not long before we got used even to this. Our daily routine was in no way affected, except that we would, from time to time, take refuge under the table, and retire into corners away from glass windows. But this, to the children, very soon became another kind of game.

Lilibet, in common with her parents and Mr Churchill, was a troublesome number in an air raid. She wanted to look. '*Do let me see what is happening,*' she would beg, her eyes very large. I often had to shout at her to come away from windows.

I started a series of parties which we called clump parties, to which I invited all the young officers I could find. The Duchess of Kent would come over. We had an equal number of young men and girls, and played hide-and-seek and sardines. We had wonderful treasure hunts, with rhyming clues and prizes.

We had the Madrigal Society every Thursday, and they all sang well. The officers joined in, and we reached quite a high standard. Some of the boys from Eton College came, and occasionally the Eton choir.

Otherwise, outings were few and far between. An occasional visit to Coppins, for tea with the Duchess of Kent and her children, or over to the small village of Holyport for riding lessons, were the chief excitements of those days. Most of the time we were high and dry, beleaguered in our Castle. Those were trying months for everyone. We were more anxious and strained than we realized. The Queen, who had a great deal to do for the King, lost that gentle look, and her mouth grew firmer. Coupon problems forced her to change her former charming style of dress.

I was on holiday when Buckingham Palace was bombed. I saw a newsreel in Scotland showing the walls of my bedroom all down, and a housemaid looking out of a broken window. The swimming pool, the children's greatest delight, was shattered. The Palace was built with two wings; on the right the swimming pool, on the left, the chapel. There was a direct hit on the Palace, and the King and Queen were both there at the time. They had, as usual, not gone to their shelter as they were supposed to do when a raid was on, but had remained together in their sitting room. It was never officially announced what a narrow escape they had, but we who knew of it were horrified, and I think they were probably prevailed upon to take more care of themselves in future as, after that, they went to the shelter more regularly when there was an alarm.

'Almost before the wreckage had cooled off,' someone told me, 'here they were, the two of them. Calmly making their way about it, like people crossing a river on stepping-stones!'

We carried on with our Guiding all through the war, and had our headquarters at the mausoleum. There is a tree sanctuary in the grounds of Windsor Castle, which was built by Queen Victoria in memory of the Prince Consort. Queen Victoria's summerhouse is close by, and we made use of that, also, for our Guide camp. Queen Victoria, I believe, used to drive over in her little pony cart and sometimes have her breakfast there. It has a big front room furnished with her favourite Scottish pine. The walls had a paper covering with green ivy design on it, very old-fashioned but rather charming. There is a large writing-table there, and an easy-chair which the Queen used in her old age. Along the passage, brass rings are let into the wall. I was told these were for her to hold on to when she was very old, for she was always extremely independent and liked to do things for herself. Her hand basin and water jug, which she kept there to wash her hands, still stand on their old-fashioned table.

Another building we made use of was a small sham temple, also built by Queen Victoria, who put up a great many of these all about the woods and gardens. One came in very useful as a boathouse for our Sea Rangers. We kept a dinghy moored outside it, on the lake. One day there had been a thunderstorm and we arrived to find the boat full of water. As we could not find the bailer, we explored the temple until we found a certain domestic article with V. R. on it, not usually mentioned in polite society. This we used as a bailer.

To my horror I saw the King coming, and in my excitement I dropped the article into the lake. It showed up in a sort of ellipse, wobbling in the water.

'What on earth are you all laughing at?' demanded the King. Dumbly we pointed. His Majesty looked down, saw this object resting on the bottom, and roared with laughter himself. I had to roll up my sleeve and get down to fishing it out.

When we were camping out, I slept in the summerhouse. I never cared much for sleeping under canvas, nor did Lilibet. She was immensely tactful about this, and never actually refused, but there always seemed to be some very good reason why she should not do so. I felt much sympathy for her. She was getting older, and had been brought up so much alone, I could understand why she did not want to undress before a lot of other children all of a sudden, and spend the night with them.

Margaret, who was much younger, thoroughly enjoyed it all. She had her own flea bag, or sleeping-bag, of which she was extremely proud, and she was a menace to the Guides officer in charge. Every evening I would watch the same performance. From the tent that housed Margaret there would burst forth storms of giggles. The Guides officer would appear, say a few well-chosen words, and retreat. The ensuing silence would reign for a minute or two, then a fresh outburst probably meant Margaret was giving her companions an imitation of the Guides officer's lecture.

Sleeping out came to an end with the arrival of the doodle-bugs, or buzz-bombs. The Queen felt it was too dangerous to have the responsibility of other people's children there, at night. So the camp became a day-time institution only, and everyone came over early in the morning, but went to their own homes at night. We had some deep slit trenches made near our camping-ground, close to the mausoleum, and an ARP man was told off to keep in touch with the wardens up at the Castle, so that we would get plenty of warning if any-thing happened to be coming along our way. The warning they had arranged was a loud tootling on the horn of a car that was kept near the listening-post. As soon as we heard it, we dropped whatever we were doing and bundled into the trench. It always seemed to happen at lunch-time, when we were very hungry and the lunch smelled extra good. There we would have to crouch in our deep trench, watching the soup and other things gradually cool off in the distance.

The King and Queen frequently came to tea with us on Sundays. The evacuee children enjoyed all this very much. All the children now had bicycles, and we used to hold grand bicycle rallies.

From the windows of Windsor Castle we would often hear the Guides talking to the soldiers who were going round the terraces to see the sights. The little girls' vegetable gardens, where they painstakingly grew lettuce, cabbage, and beans, were a favourite visiting-place, and one day we heard a Guide say, pointing up to the drawing room window:

'And in there is where the two Princesses have their danc-ing lessons and do taproom dancing!'

While we were at Windsor about twelve of us worked for our Guides' cooking badge. We met each Thursday from two to four in the housekeeper's kitchen. Each had a baking-board and rolling-pin. The Princesses loved it. We used to send up the result of our efforts – stews and soups and cakes – to the ARP men on the look-out on the Castle walls. Occasionally on Cake Day we held a tea-party for the officers next door in the housekeeper's dining room. This was most popular. We gave them the scones and cakes still hot from the oven, which must have been most indigestible.

There were changes everywhere. The familiar and loved servants who had served Their Majesties so long, and seemed like members of the family themselves, began to leave, called up to serve in factories or in women's services. And, like everyone else, we were understaffed, and the most unlikely people had to take a hand with the most domestic jobs. It was now that the King's piper, who before had never done anything but pipe, started to help by waiting at table. Several retired pages, grown old, came back to do what they could.

At this time my ambition was to join the WRNS. I felt I ought not to be shut up in Windsor Castle, but all the household said I was doing my job of work by keeping these young children happy so that the King and Queen would be free as far as they could be to think about the affairs of State. However, I was duly registered. I remember being asked, 'Who is your employer?' and I replied, 'Her Majesty the Queen,' which they put down rather unbelievingly.

I waited for papers to arrive, but none did. I mentioned it to the King and Queen one day that I had registered. The Queen said, 'Oh, I have had to register too!' I said I rather fancied myself in the WRNS, and the King said, 'What you are doing is your job. We could not carry on if you weren't here.' And he added, 'Besides, you would only be cooking some old admiral's breakfast.'

From the time Lilibet was fifteen she began to take on social tasks. The King made her Colonel of the Grenadier Guards in 1942, which was a great delight to her. It was a popular appointment, for we had seen a great deal of the Guards all through our Windsor years, and both girls had many friends among the young officers.

Lilibet took her duties with immense seriousness and zeal. It was the first time she had done anything of the kind. Like all young people, in her enthusiasm she almost overdid it. After one inspection, at which Lilibet had made some rather pointed criticisms in her ringing voice, one of the majors said to me, laughing:

'Crawfie, you should tell the Princess quietly that the first requisite of a really good officer is to be able to temper justice with mercy.'

Philip appeared on the scene again. It was quite a time since we had seen him. We were all involved in one of the panto-mimes, very excited just before our first performance, when Lilibet came to me, looking rather pink. 'Who *do* you think is coming to see us act, Crawfie? Philip.'

He had been in the Navy for some time, and I wondered what he would be like now he was grown up. He was, I knew, to sit in the front row, and I took a moment off to have a look at him. He was greatly changed. It was a grave and charming young man who sat there, with nothing of the rather bump-tious boy I had first known about him now. He looked more than ever, I thought, like a Viking, weather-beaten and strained, and his manners left nothing to be desired.

The pantomime went off very well. I have never known Lilibet more animated. There was a sparkle about her none of us had ever seen before. Many people remarked on it. From then on, the two young people began to correspond. She took an immense interest in him, and where he was, and on what ship. At that time, most girls had someone they wrote to at sea, or at the front. I think just at the start she liked to be able to say that she, too, was sending off an occasional parcel, and writing letters to a man who was fighting for his country.

Although she was now growing up and taking on a number of outside duties, Princess Elizabeth still had no suite of her own. She divided her time between the schoolroom and the nursery, and as now, from time to time, people came to see her officially, it was decided that she must have a sitting room of her own.

There was a little boudoir done in pink tapestry between the schoolroom and her bedroom which had once been the

Princess Royal's sitting room. This she could use as her private apartment. Lilibet was enchanted with the idea, and we moved out a lot of books and had the room made ready for her, with one or two more comfortable chairs. This was her first real break-away from nursery and schoolroom life. When we went back to the Palace after the war she had her own suite of rooms there – a bedroom and sitting room and bathroom, just along the corridor from Margaret's rooms and mine.

Like most other families we, too, were plunged suddenly into mourning. We heard news of the Duke of Kent's tragic death. The aircraft in which he was travelling on duty ran into the hillside in a desolate part of Scotland.

It was a great shock to the two little girls. It was the second uncle they had lost completely, for though the first, Uncle David, was not dead, they did not see him any more. The royal conspiracy of silence had closed about him as it did about so many other uncomfortable things. In the Palace and the Castle, his name was never mentioned.

The news had to be broken to the Duchess over the telephone where she was at home, the last baby still very new. For a long time she was prostrate, and she has never regained the old brightness and gaiety that were once hers. Her very lovely face to me is now always a little sad.

For years she went nowhere and did nothing, devoting herself entirely to her three children. The youngest was only seven weeks old when the Duke died. I have always found it a little sad to see this exceptionally beautiful young woman leading, as she now does, such a quiet life.

A year after the Duke's death she went up to Scotland, taking a friend with her. She sought out the keeper who had found the crashed plane. It had come down in a very desolate and inaccessible spot, miles across the moors from anywhere, and very rough going.

On foot she made her pilgrimage to the spot, and sat for a little while there on a boulder, alone. One can picture the thoughts and memories of their happy times together that must have gone through her mind there among the heather he had loved so much, the curlews crying overhead.

CHAPTER IX

V Day and the Return to London

As far as the Royal Family were aware, my private life was entirely made up of visits to my mother during holidays, and I am sure it never occurred to any of them that I had ever thought of marrying. This was by no means surprising, as I had never given a soul the slightest indication of such a possibility, and I was determined that no one was going to be worried or upset by even the vaguest hint.

Sometimes I was asked point-blank by friends if I was going to remain unmarried and stay with the Royal Family all my life, but such queries were easily parried.

However, the time came in 1939, after the war had started, for me to make a very hard decision, but, although it was a great effort, I made my decision to postpone the idea of marriage until after the war.

To be honest, my conscience worried me considerably and it seemed to me that, if I married now that the war was on, I would feel like a soldier who had deserted his post. The King and Queen relied on me. I was entirely in charge of the two Princesses, one of whom was the heir presumptive to the throne of England, and it gave their parents, who themselves carried such crushing responsibilities, considerable peace of mind so long as I remained with the Princesses.

So duty won the battle, and I waited until after the war before getting married. But I know I was right in my decision, and the very happy life I now enjoy is ample repayment.

Lilibet registered when she was sixteen, along with other girls of her own age-group, at the Labour Exchange in Windsor.

From that moment she agitated to be allowed to join one of the women's services. 'I ought to do as other girls of my age do,' she said firmly. Many of her friends had already gone. Her cousin, Lady Mary Cambridge, was a VAD (Voluntary Aid Detachment), working not in some luxurious hospital for officers where her presence would have been more than welcomed, but in the poorest parts of blitzed London, where she did a wonderful job.

There was little doubt now that Lilibet was England's future Queen. No one ever spoke of this. But I think perhaps it was in the King's mind more than anyone knew, and that it was because of this he was at first very reluctant to allow her to join up and face what could not help being a certain amount of danger and hazard.

Finally he gave way. Both his daughters could be immensely persuasive, and had a habit of getting what they wanted in the end. Especially from their father. After some discussion with his advisers, it was decided the Princess would be allowed to join the Auxiliary Territorial Service as a subaltern. So Commandant Wellesley arrived one morning, very brisk and hearty, and took Lilibet in hand. At the depot a car jacked up, its wheels off, awaited her. In the following weeks she was put through the whole business of taking an engine to bits and putting it together again.

There was great excitement when her uniform came. She was very proud of it, and I think the King in his own heart was very proud of his daughter for having taken this stand. Margaret was much too young to join up, and as usual she was very cross at seeing Lilibet do something without her. But when she saw how very unbecoming khaki was, I think it made her feel much better.

I took Margaret one day to tea at Lilibet's mess in Camberley, which was a great treat for her. It was amusing to see how hearty all the lady officers were, drinking sherry and smoking cigarettes. Lilibet has never smoked and does not do so now. Nor has she ever adopted the fashion of blood-red nails, but paints hers only a very pale pink.

Commandant Wellesley used to come at eleven every morning and say, 'Do you think the Princess will be able to do this, or do that?' I had always been inclined to keep her in bed with a cold, and one day Alah came to me at breakfast and asked if I would ring the commandant and say the Princess was not well enough to come.

I went along to see her.

'Oh, Crawfie,' she said, 'I simply must go.'

I said, 'But don't you realize what a responsibility and a nuisance you will be to everyone, and how much you will worry them? What good can you do, going along there if you are not well?'

I rang up the commandant and we discussed this. She said that the Princess had already overtired herself because she was so keen. She had gone through the most arduous things at times when other girls would have been only too glad of an excuse to slack and take things easy.

'Tell the Princess she must remain in bed until she is really fit,' the commandant said.

Princess Elizabeth always had that will to carry on in all circumstances, just as the King had done until he became really ill and unable to continue in 1948. He had insisted on keeping up his schedule, using his human body when somebody else would have given up years before; in fact, harming himself in order to carry on.

On the day of her last test the King and Queen came down to see her. A smudged face looked up from under a car, very grave and determined to get good marks and do the right thing. She took immense pride in the fact that she was doing what other girls of her age had to do, and apart from coming back to Windsor to sleep, she kept strictly to the routine of the mess, taking her turn with the others as duty officer, doing inspections, and working really hard on the maintenance of cars. She was a very junior officer, and had to salute her seniors along with the rest. She went right through the course. It was not until a year later, when she had passed all her tests, that she was promoted, and even then she was one of the most junior officers in the mess.

She was efficient, neat, and quick. Presently she drove me round Windsor Park to show me what she could do. Every morning she drove the commandant over to the ATS depot at Camberley. I don't think, in those days of sudden air raids and bomb dropping, Commandant Wellesley altogether relished her responsibility.

Margaret's envy when she watched her sister drive a big Red Cross van away one morning burst out once again, and she was resentful at having to spend her day in the schoolroom with all those exciting things going on elsewhere.

'I was born too late,' she stormed one day angrily. I remember laughing and saying, 'The day will come when you will not think that.'

Lilibet passed all her driving tests, and there came the triumphant autumn day when she drove all through the heavy war-time traffic of London, up the Great West Road, along Piccadilly, and down the Mall in the blackout, into Buckingham Palace, to show her parents her achievement. The beaming policeman threw the gates open for her. She has always been very popular with all members of the staff.

None of us ever owned how anxious were some of our moments when the sirens went off and we knew she was out, and awaited her return.

It taught her a great deal besides the driving and oiling of motor-cars. She got from her life in the mess a glimpse she would probably never have had of another side of life.

One day she said to me, 'Crawfie, Aunt Mary is coming down on an inspection, and you've no idea what a business it has been. Everyone working so hard – spit and polish the whole day long. Now I realize what must happen when Papa and Mummie go anywhere. That's something I shall never forget.'

Under the Regency Act, Lilibet had to act as a Councillor of State in the event of the King's absence or illness, although she was not yet officially of age. It was a solemn office for so young a girl – she was now seventeen – and she was soon to be called on to exercise her office.

In 1944 the King went to Italy. He flew there. It was top secret. No one at all outside the family circle was told. I never knew, and although both the children did, they never told me or anyone else. Both keep secrets with absolute trustworthiness. Later I heard that the servants had guessed there was something up after seeing the King's tailor arrive with a box marked 'Tropical Kit'.

It was an anxious time for everyone while he was away. Lilibet used to say, comforting herself, 'But General Alexander has promised faithfully to take care of him.'

While the King was away, a murder case came up in which a reprieve was granted. Lilibet had to sign it, along with the Queen and the other Councillors of State. After her sheltered life in the Palace, this sudden coming up against the grim and sordid made a great impression on her.

'What makes people do such terrible things, Crawfie?' she

said, discussing it with me afterwards. 'One ought to know. There should be some way to help them. I have so much to learn about people!'

At that time I remember being afraid that, surrounded as she had been by so much that was tragic and depressing in the most impressionable years of her life, she would lose her brightness and that love of fun all young people ought to have.

And then, like the sudden blowing away of a storm, the atmosphere lightened. It was as if quite suddenly the sun came out again after years of gloom. Victory was in the air. We began to wait for the daily papers with new hope and excitement. Things were happening. Everyone rushed to his room for the one o'clock news. Rocket bombs falling in Windsor Great Park had brought the war right on to our doorstep – and then, suddenly, it was all over. The wireless bulletins began to read like penny dreadfuls, and the newspapers were full of pictures of German leaders' suicides. There were so many rumours flying around one hardly knew what to believe among so much that was scarcely believable.

Then came Sunday, 6 May, anniversary of the accession of King George V. The King and Queen were at Windsor. The whole family was dressed and ready to go, as usual, to church, when there came an urgent telephone call from London asking Their Majesties to return at once. It was decided the two Princesses should go with them, and play their part in an historical occasion no one is likely ever to forget.

The war with Germany ended on 8 May. The Palace was hemmed in by a surging mob of excited people, calling for Their Majesties. There were the usual balcony appearances, this time joined by Mr Churchill. At first he stood back modestly, but the King and Queen drew him forward, and he stood there, beaming, while the crowds yelled their approval.

No one not in England at that time can realize the almost hysterical relief that came with the lessening of the awful tension we had come through. No more lying awake at night, listening. No more waking up to the early-morning sound of the sweeping up of broken glass. Hitler was dead, that ranting voice stilled for ever. Nor would we, tuning in at evening time, come across Lord Haw-Haw's oily eloquence any more. For a little while everyone was crazy with excitement. Margaret threw all her German books on the floor and announced she was not going to do any more of Hitler's language. She was fourteen, but mentally far ahead of her age. The two Princesses remained with their parents at the Palace for the peace celebrations. I went up home for a holiday again, the first for a very long time.

I was still in Scotland when final victory came on 15 August. The two Princesses wrote me, telling me all about it, and what a glorious time they had. For that night something happened that had never occurred before in Palace history. The King allowed his two daughters to go out of the gates, and among the crowds. Two Guards officers took them, and they joined the revellers outside, and called, with the rest, for the King and Queen to come out.

Now, at long last, the family could take a real holiday, could sit back and relax and for a short time let the world go by without them. I rejoined them at Balmoral towards the end of September. There was an entirely new atmosphere in the Castle. The King and Queen were both like their old selves again. They looked rested and years younger, and the King had found great amusement in having Lilibet taken out deer stalking.

As usual the clothes question was acute. There were no coupons to spare for sporting garments, and in the end Lilibet wore the plus-fours trousers of one of her father's suits. In

Scotland, King and keeper alike wear the same tweed. It is a nice neutral shade that merges easily into the background on a moor. The King has it specially woven for him.

Lilibet went off with the head keeper, who coached her in the mysterious art of seeing the stag and recognizing him before he sees you!

She loved those days on the moors and promised to become a good shot. She was so touched and pleased by the keepers' tactful care of her. They would find a big boulder at lunch-time, put her one side of it with her lunch, and themselves retire to the other side.

The Balmoral shooting lunch is always the same: a stuffed roll, a slice of plum pudding, an apple. The war-time plum pudding never had any plums in it, but anything tastes good eaten out-of-doors in the sunshine among the heather.

Just for a little while, until the first exciting novelty wore off, Lilibet was like a golfer who has holed out in one, or a fisherman who has caught a fish so large that even he has no need to lie about it. In the evenings we talked of nothing but stalking and antlers and points. We had to retrace with her, in mind, every exciting inch of the day.

Margaret felt very left out, and again resentful. She was now at a girl's most awkward age, neither quite a child nor quite grown up, and she took the interlude much harder than ever her sister had done. Perhaps because Lilibet had always been far more firmly disciplined.

However, presently Margaret conveniently decided she did not care for sporting women, thought shooting unwomanly, and never meant to do any herself. Moreover, she did not consider Papa's plus-fours looked at all nice on her sister.

Lilibet still came to me for an hour or so in the mornings for lessons, but she was growing up fast, and there were more and more claims on her time. She would not have been human had she not rather enjoyed the moment when, with a sweet smile, she departed, leaving her sister alone with the lesson books.

Margaret was rarely bored with her work. She was always a most interesting child to teach, with her quick, bright mind and amusing turn of phrase. But on those sunny mornings in Scotland her eyes would often wander towards the moors and the heather-covered hills beyond the river.

I used to read to them both in the evenings, and often out-of-doors. We read all Scott that autumn, and we had some wonderful picnics. There was a feeling of leisure about again that no one had enjoyed for years.

The Queen long before had found an abandoned little house up on the moor, and had taken it on a ninety-nine-year lease. It had once been an old schoolhouse. The kitchen had a big fireplace, and there were handy cupboards for pots and pans where we could keep our picnic gear.

This simplified life. It meant we need not drag a lot of things around with us every time. We gathered a store of firewood and heather in dry weather, and kept paper and matches there to make the fires.

The little house was never furnished. When it rained and we had to have meals inside, we – the Queen, the Princesses, the lady-in-waiting, and odd guests and myself – all sat on the floor. Jock, the Highland pony, who carried coats and the food up for us, would make brave efforts on these occasions to join us. He was very domesticated, and passionately fond of mince, or chopped-up meat.

We cooked our own food up there, or almost cooked it. The chef had a kind way of starting things for us before he packed up the baskets. Onions were a must on every picnic. We fried them ourselves. The Queen was a great hand at cutting them up ready for frying, and she had the knack of doing it without making herself weep in the process. We also had stuffed rolls, a plum cake, and ginger snaps.

When the meal was over we used to carry the pots and pans down to the burn and wash them up there. Then the Princesses would ride off together on their ponies.

That was an interlude I look back on with great pleasure. The war was over. We were not yet enveloped in the trials and many tribulations of the peace. But even here there was a shadow for the King and Queen. Alah died quite suddenly. She had gone to Sandringham for Christmas as usual. Although the children were fast growing up, the nursery life had always gone on much as usual, with Alah always there, a constant stand-by and comfort. The two Princesses often had tea with her. When no one was coming, and the family were alone, Margaret and Lilibet often had their baths early, and dined by the nursery fire in their dressing-gowns and bedroom slippers, listening to their favourite wireless programme. Probably *Itma*.

Alah, like her royal master and mistress, would never own to feeling ill, but we had all seen that she was not looking well, and that ordinary tasks, of which she had once made nothing, were suddenly an effort to her.

It was a great shock to the Queen, who lost a very dear and understanding friend, one who had been with her since babyhood and who, by her association over so many years, had become a part of the family. It is a gap which, today, cannot be filled.

Alah was buried at her own home, in Hertfordshire, near St Paul's, Waldenbury, where she had originally joined the Strathmore family to nurse the Queen, then a baby.

On the coffin there was laid a wreath made entirely of violets, with a card bearing the words, 'In Loving and Thankful Memory. Elizabeth R.'

Prince Philip was abroad. We did not see him again that summer, but I knew Lilibet wrote to him and he to her, and her parents were also aware of it, and nothing was said. Then one day I suddenly became aware that she had his picture on her mantelpiece.

'Is that altogether wise? A number of people come and go,' I pointed out. 'You know what that will lead to. People will begin all sorts of gossip about you.'

She looked at the photograph for a moment thoughtfully. 'Oh, dear, I suppose they will,' she said, and she laughed rather ruefully.

The next time I went into her room the picture had disappeared. In its place there was another one. It was still of Philip, but this time completely ambushed behind the enormous fair beard he had managed to raise while he was at sea during the war.

'There you are, Crawfie. I defy anyone to recognize who that is,' said Lilibet. 'He's completely incognito in that one.'

The disguise was a good one, but it was not good enough. Those oddly piercing, intent blue eyes were much too individual. In the end, what I had expected took place. The first early rumours began to get around outside the Palace, the whispers and the stories began. Presently one paper came right out into the open and announced it was Prince Philip of Greece whose photograph the Princess kept in her room.

About now, Lilibet was getting her first grown-up clothes. She had had very little new during the war, and few households can have done a better job in mend and make-do than the royal household did. And even in her first grown-up outfit, Lilibet had several of her mother's evening dresses made over for her.

Now for the first time she was permitted to choose some clothes for herself; with the help of the indefatigable Mr Norman Hartnell. Lilibet's taste in clothes followed her mother's closely. She chose mostly pastel shades, and was from the first very attached to silk or thin wool frocks, with coats that matched exactly. For evening frocks she mostly chooses very full skirts of the picture kind. Wisely, for these suit her admirably.

All Lilibet's clothes were handed on to Margaret. There is no waste whatever in the royal household. Far from resenting this inheritance of wardrobe, Margaret was always delighted to have her sister's frocks, and above all her pretty tweeds. She was never quite so enthusiastic about the hats, and was very angry when one astute woman journalist noted and photographed her wearing a hat that had been Lilibet's, and added a caption drawing attention to the fact.

I think there was less friction between these two than is usual between sisters. Probably this is due to Lilibet's really unusually lovely nature. All her feeling for her pretty sister was motherly and protective. She hated Margaret to be left out; she hated her antics to be misunderstood. In her own intuitive fashion I think she saw ahead how later on Margaret was bound to be misrepresented and misunderstood. How often in earlier days have I heard her cry in real anguish, 'Stop her, Mummie. Oh, please stop her,' when Margaret was being more than usually preposterous and amusing and outrageous. Though Lilibet, with the rest of us, laughed at Margaret's antics – and indeed it was impossible not to – I think they often made her uneasy and filled her with foreboding. On more than one occasion the official camera has caught her giving Margaret a nudge and a sisterly look that has said plainer than any words, 'Margaret. Please behave!' or 'You must *not* laugh here.'

Lilibet enjoyed buying her first grown-up clothes very much. The dressmakers would first bring sketches, and then models of the gowns chosen, which would be shown her worn by Mr Hartnell's *svelte* young ladies. I persuaded her to get a cherry-red dinner dress, as this was a colour that brought out her lovely complexion. She chose one with a tight-fitting jacket made of thick silk, piped with white, and a pleated skirt, and this I always considered to be one of the most becoming frocks she ever had.

Lilibet never took the keen interest in clothes that Margaret does. Margaret at an early age would draw little sketches of beautifully dressed ladies with sylphlike figures, and pictures of frocks she would have liked to have for herself. Excellent designs some of them were, too. There are so many things Margaret could have done with brilliance and distinction.

Peace turned out to be not very peaceful. There were changes everywhere. A change of government put an entirely new set of people in the news, and official parties produced a number of unfamiliar faces. Mr Attlee became Prime Minister and it seemed strange to see him in place of Mr Churchill. I particularly remember in those days what an impression Mr Aneurin Bevan's shirts and cuff-links made on me! He never wears court or evening dress, but he has the most beautifully tailored silk shirts, and the most magnificent cuff-links of anyone in London.

I never knew what the King and Queen made of these changes. They never spoke of them. Even I, who had lived so long on close terms with them, never had any inkling as to whom they themselves liked or disliked. In the Palace, discretion and self-control – and I feel I must add genuine self-sacrifice – are carried to lengths quite unbelievable to the world outside. Their Majesties are above politics.

But the changes were to come still nearer home. There arose murmurings and mutterings inside the Palace itself. There also, a new and strange element had crept in. During and just after the war, the servant problem became at the Palace, as everywhere else, an acute one. Poor Ainslie had many problems. He aged under our eyes, coping with them all. In happier days, he never had had to look far for staff; it just came, like the flowers in springtime! There was always someone whose butler had a son just growing up, the height of whose ambition was to become one of the Palace staff. There was always someone's housekeeper who put in an application for her daughter before the child had even left school.

This supply dried up completely. Ainslie, for the first time, had to join the endless queues at the register offices and compete with newly-made millionaires who offered far higher wages. That, he told me ruefully, meant that you never really knew whom you were getting in. There was no longer the old family tradition. The happy days of Baily and Pottinger, who had worked in the Palace all their lives and had no existence apart from it, had come to an end. Everyone now was as good as everyone else.

Today the staff is well housed. Where many years ago they inhabited the beetle-ridden basements where even I found it hard to stand upright, each housemaid now has a private bedroom. There is a coal fire they can light whenever they want to.

The King has to keep a very large staff to cope with the size of the Palace, and the incessant entertaining that is a part of his job. There is a housekeeper who runs the house and looks after the housemaids, of whom there are usually about fifty permanent ones, mostly country girls. Many come from Aberdeen, recruited when the family is at Balmoral. Some come from the estate at Glamis.

The male staff is under the steward of the Palace, my old friend Ainslie of the early Windsor days. He superintends a regular army of footmen, butlers, pages, chefs, coal porters, to say nothing of the already mentioned Vermin Man, and a table decker, and the clock winder.

Some of the servants have marvellous and dignified titles. There is the Yeoman of the Gold Pantry, who looks after the gold plate that is used only on very formal occasions. There is the Yeoman of the Silver Pantry, who is in charge of all the silver. Daily a fleet of charladies arrive in the early hours and clean the endless basements. After them come the housemaids, who also arise at an unearthly hour and, like ministering spirits, are never seen again until six in the evening, when they reappear to draw the curtains and turn down the beds.

Besides the Vermin Man with his traps, both sticky and orthodox, a small, determined man came in weekly to wind the clocks. He just walked in as a matter of course, no matter what happened to be going on at the time, and attended to his job. He was impersonal as a bluebottle on a windowpane, and no one ever took the slightest notice of him.

Then there was the table decker. He came daily to fill up the flower vases all over the Palace, and to renew the flowers. His name was Mr Linnett. Like the clock winder, he just came in and did his job, and went again. He never took any notice of anyone, and no one took any notice of him.

The Queen liked to have lots of flowers about her. Her rooms were always full of them, wherever we happened to be. The scent of roses always brings her back very clearly to me, still.

The Queen has two dressers, and there are always three special housemaids to do the royal apartments. It is a definite distinction, much sought after, to be promoted to work on this floor. The King has two valets. In the old days, a special footman and housemaid took care of the nursery quarters.

At one time staff meals were served in the steward's room and servants' hall. But a new arrangement was made not long ago. The entire staff were put on board wages – they are paid more, but feed themselves, with their own kitchens on the top floor. Only the upper servants feed together in the steward's

room, presided over by Ainslie. Besides all these, there are
innumerable men and women clerks who work in the Palace
offices. For them there is a clerks' dining room. The King's
family is a large one!

The servants are always very interested in the Princesses. I
often caught groups of them waiting in the passages in hopes
of catching a glimpse of the little girls. When there is any kind
of function, everyone who wishes to may come and see the
Royal Family dressed and ready. Mrs Evans, who used to be
housekeeper at the Palace but has now retired, always
received an invitation from the Queen, when there was anything special like the opening of Parliament. Her Majesty's
personal maid would invite the dressmakers, and perhaps
some of the girls who had sewed the dresses. The children
always had to come down, for they took a great delight in
seeing Mummie dressed. So I always got a private view also.
The King is charming at these times. He likes to have people
admire his Queen. He would stand and look at her, and say to
us, 'How do you like the dress? Don't you think the hat is just
a little too much up?' (Or down.)

Odd Victorian customs remained in force at the Palace. It
was not the thing to cross the courtyard in front of the Palace
carrying parcels. Lilibet had for a time a lady-in-waiting who
was rather a Bohemian young person. She was married, and
had a small flat in London which she had to run without any
help. So she used to do her household shopping on her way to
the Palace and stuff the results in a basket on her bicycle
handle-bars. One morning Lilibet and I were looking out of
the sitting room window when the Queen joined us. The lady-
in-waiting, plus bicycle and basket, had just arrived below.
Her attire was not of the most conventional, and she wore a
scarf tied over her hair.

The Queen took a step forward and peered out of the
window. 'Lilibet, darling! Surely that's not —. You must speak

to her. She really can't come here like that! She must wear a hat.'

Lilibet said patiently, 'Don't be old-fashioned, Mummie. These days girls simply don't *have* a hat.'

Margaret continued her regular daily lessons with me up to the time she departed for South Africa with her father and mother in 1947. She was then sixteen, highly strung and not very strong, and many people doubted the wisdom of including her in this strenuous undertaking. I have often thought she would have been better left at home. But she, too, was growing up, and becoming more and more determined not to be left out of things. She usually got her own way in the end.

Lilibet had done with lessons altogether except for her music. This she kept up. Both of them play the piano well and sing nicely, Margaret with a real touch of genius that would have taken her, under different circumstances, a very long way indeed.

Lilibet now attended Council meetings, went about with her mother, did more and more visiting and going about by herself; and discussed State affairs most days with her father. By now the important part she would one day have to play in the world was officially recognized. This became obvious when she got her own flag with her special coat of arms, her secretary, and her lady-in-waiting.

Mr Churchill, his hands full enough already, often found opportunity when at the Palace to discuss the general situation at length with this young girl. The advice and counsel he gave Lilibet then from his vast wisdom and experience must have been of inestimable value to her. The fact that this very great statesman found time to do this in the midst of his other responsibilities must have done much to bring home to her how important a part she was some day to have to take in her country's affairs.

Mr Churchill had a very nice way with young people, and both the Princesses were devoted to him. When they were with him, they were all eyes.

The usual morning visit with Mummie and Papa had been resumed after the war. The two Princesses still had nursery breakfast together right up to the day of Lilibet's wedding. But now at ten o'clock, while Margaret was busy with me, Lilibet would ring for her lady-in-waiting and deal with her own correspondence and see her dressmaker. Most afternoons she would either open some bazaar or visit factories or hospitals. She always managed to find a little while to go into the garden with the dogs, and mostly I joined her.

I felt now that my job was to provide a little light relief for Lilibet. Her days were so full of functions and duties that cannot have been other than oppressive for a girl of nineteen. We started the madrigal classes again, and now we got together thirty or forty young people. They came into the Bow Room, and after singing we had sherry and biscuits.

Among the girls there was a charming little person with pretty manners, named Jennifer Bevan. She was to become a close friend of Margaret's, and her first lady-in-waiting.

Margaret was a voracious reader. She read anything she got her hands on. I believed in letting the Princesses read and read and read. There were dozens of comics, and when they grew out of the comics they took the women's magazines and other periodicals. They have read a great many of the classics, and have a good grounding in literature.

Margaret always has had a flare for beautiful words. She is innately artistic and always puts the proper word in the proper place without any effort.

❖

Lilibet now had her own suite and household at the Palace, which really meant that one of the housemaids and a footman made it their particular duty to look after her.

Her bedroom was pink and fawn, with flowered chintz and plain white furniture. Nothing at all magnificent or ornate. She never took a very personal interest in furnishings or decorations, the way Margaret did. She tended to accept gratefully anything that was done for her, and settle down happily in a sitting room arranged by someone else.

This has been done so often at the Palace, where there is so much of everything already, though most of it is appallingly out of date. With mounds and mounds of furniture around already, furnishing a room tends to mean adapting things. It would be extravagant to buy more. So it boils down to re-arranging a few whatnots and valuable antiques that would be wonderful in a museum but are somewhat depressing in a private apartment. One of the subjects Alah and I agreed on wholeheartedly was one day voiced by her as we moved out of sight some truly amazing candlesticks.

'What we need here, Miss Crawford,' she said grimly, 'is one really good fire.'

Lilibet's dressing-table was always simplicity itself, and a picture of order. She never left much lying about. Like her father, she is neat and methodical beyond words. A small table by her bed held the books she was reading at the time. Both girls read largely, and the latest novels, accompanied by at least one slightly 'heavier' book, were kept on hand. From the seat at her dressing-table, Lilibet had a wonderful view towards Big Ben.

'No wonder you are always so punctual,' Margaret said one day tartly, 'you can't very well help it.'

On wet days when we could not get out, Margaret would say, 'Let's explore.' Then we would wander off round the Palace, to the war-scarred and shut-off apartments where the workmen were busy. During the war the glass chandeliers had all been removed for safety, the pictures and ornaments packed away. Now they were back, waiting to be unpacked and returned to their places, and sometimes we took a hand. It was fun undoing the beautiful crystal pieces and china figures. There was no saying what we might find next. We polished with our handkerchiefs the bits we unpacked. Often as she worked, Margaret would sing in what she called her 'village-choir voice'. This caused considerable amazement among the workmen who passed by.

And one day, pottering through the half-dismantled rooms, we came upon a very old piano. Margaret was delighted with this find. She dragged up a packing-case, sat down and proceeded to play Chopin. As she touched the notes, great clouds of dust flew out.

Margaret makes everything personal to herself. Her room is done over in salmon-pink that to me at once suggests Margaret. In the centre of her room she has a large round table on which can always be found a lavish clutter. Letters, invitations, dance programmes, greetings telegrams – in short, a hoosh-mi. Her white wooden dressing-table is littered with bottles, manicure instruments, and small ornaments. Anything small, neat, and miniature has always had an immense appeal to Margaret, so *petite* herself.

Both girls have a series of lace-and-net-trimmed covers or clothes tidies, a custom they learned from their mother, and one that other girls might with advantage copy. The Queen's clothes would be folded and put out ready for her, and the silk-and-net cover thrown over them. When her maid took her clothes to be ironed or mended over her arm, there would always be one of these tidily covering them. Nothing was ever left lying about, or hanging over the back of a chair, or dropped on the floor.

❖

Margaret was a great one for practical jokes. More than once I have seen an equerry put his hand into his pocket, and find it, to his amazement, full of sticky lime balls. I am sure the last person ever suspected was the demure-looking little girl at the other end of the table. Shoes left outside doors would become inexplicably filled up with acorns. Once, when a new secretary had arrived, and been honoured with Margaret's attention, she had sudden qualms after she was in bed.

'Oh, Crawfie, perhaps I shouldn't have done that. *Do* go down and take them out.' I said I would do nothing of the kind, but later I rang through to the equerry and asked him if he could do anything about it. He was very much amused, but thought perhaps Margaret hadn't chosen a very good person to play a joke on, and he got them removed.

I never told Margaret what I had done. For some days she watched her victim, anxious to see whether he looked at all cross with her, and whenever he was around she would sit there looking too good to be true!

Lilibet had learned to drive during her ATS training, and the King gave her a car of her own, for her twenty-first birthday. She had longed to have one for some time, and she was immensely proud of it, and her special number, HRH 1. People in London soon got to know it, and looked out for her, and gave her a cheer.

After that, Margaret had to learn. Lilibet taught her when they were up at Balmoral. The moorland roads and empty lanes of Scotland are an excellent place for a beginner. Margaret took her driving test like everyone else. She took it in Ballater, the nearest town in which a driving inspector was to be found. He told us Margaret drove very well, with judgement and skill. When I left the Palace she was still trying to persuade the King to let her have a car of her own, but she had not succeeded. But she drove the royal cars. Once when she was going away for a weekend, in the King's Daimler, she tapped at the window as soon as they got out of the Castle grounds, told the chauffeur to come and sit inside with her maid. She herself climbed into the driving seat beside the detective. The chauffeur wasn't at all sure he ought to let her drive the King's car, but what could he do? Moreover, he was extremely embarrassed at having to sit in the back of the royal car like that, but any nervousness he may have felt soon went, for he realized the wheel was in capable hands.

When they arrived at their destination the car door was thrown ceremoniously open by her hostess's footman, who expected the Princess to alight. Out came, instead, the maid and the chauffeur.

CHAPTER X

Elizabeth and Philip

L IKE so many girls who grew up in the war years, Lilibet never had any proper coming out. She just started, quietly, going to parties from time to time, with her personal friends.

I tried to encourage Lilibet, presently, to give little cocktail parties of her own, in her own sitting room, to return the hospitality of her many friends. I could never get her to do this. She was too accustomed to leaving it all to Mummie. Mummie always had done all the entertaining, and the habit was hard to break. Then, one day, Lilibet came to my room, her eyes very bright.

'Crawfie! Someone is coming tonight!' she said half shyly.

Prince Philip was back from abroad.

The three of them had dinner together in Lilibet's sitting room, and later romped in the corridor. It is difficult, looking back on it, to remember the sequence of events. I noticed, suddenly, that Lilibet began to take more trouble with her appearance, that it seemed to matter more to her what she wore at this evening party or that. Then I would find that Philip had been there!

And I noticed that suddenly she began to play her gramophone more than usual, and that her favourite tune of the moment was 'People Will Say We're in Love', from the musical show *Oklahoma!* They had been to that show together, and Lilibet would often ask the band at the various restaurants where they dined and danced to play this tune for her. She and Philip rarely danced together. They had to be so discreet. But one can picture the glances they exchanged as they passed on the dance floor, each with another partner.

Philip I now liked immensely. It was obvious to all of us that he was very much in love, I think had been ever since they met at our last pantomime, and they began writing to each other. In those lonely months at sea he must have thought of her a great deal, and he must have weighed, too, his own situation. Though there would be great advantages in such a union, for him there would also be great disadvantages.

He must often have thought of Prince Albert, another Prince Consort, who had found that role no bed of roses. Philip had been educated at Gordonstoun, where tactful subjugation had been no part of his training, and there must have been moments when he wondered whether he could possibly face it.

But he loved her very much. He was a forthright and completely natural young man, given to say what he thought. There was nothing of the polished courtier about him. He came into the Palace like a refreshing sea breeze. I often saw him wandering around in his shirt sleeves.

Presently he began to come up as a matter of course, and have dinner informally, in the old comfortable nursery fashion, in the old nursery, which Margaret now used as her sitting room. The food was of the simplest. Fish, some sort of sweet, and orangeade. Philip does not smoke and drinks very little.

After dinner, there would be high jinks in the corridors. Philip removed from the door the old card with 'Nursery' on it, and substituted another marked 'Maggie's Playroom'. They would play ball (a good many electric-light bulbs suffered) and race about like a bunch of high-spirited children. It was always a threesome, unless I took a hand and did something about it by removing Margaret on some pretext or other. I felt the constant presence of the little sister, who was far from undemanding, and liked to have a good bit of attention herself, was not helping on the romance much.

Margaret was fond of Philip in an entirely sisterly fashion, and he was very good for her. He stood no nonsense. She was then at adolescence's most tiresome stage, apt at times to be comically regal and overgracious, and Philip wasn't having any. She would dilly-dally outside the lift, keeping everyone waiting, until Philip, losing patience, would give her a good push that settled the question of precedence quite simply.

Everyone in the household was by now aware of what was in the air. One could not see the young people together without realizing what they felt for each other. But what her father and mother, the King and Queen, thought about it we had not the slightest idea.

Now the newspapers began to speculate about the royal romance, and wherever they went a thousand eyes watched them. It must have been torture to both of them. One day Lilibet came back rather excited from visiting a factory. I hurried to her room to see what was wrong.

'Crawfie, it was horrible,' she said. 'They shouted at me, "Where's Philip?"'

It was a coarse piece of thoughtlessness on the part of those who apparently had never paused to consider the feelings of a very young girl, sensitive and in love, but not as yet engaged. How could she be sure she would find a response in the heart of the man she loved, to what was in her own? He had not yet spoken to her. In the months that followed they were both to have much to put up with. The heart of a princess is shy and as easily hurt as any other young girl's heart. In time royalty grow accustomed and hardened to this prying into their private lives, and make little of it. But not at nineteen. Not in love, deeply and passionately, for the first time.

It spoiled for them both days that should have been care-free and happy. She began to dread the trips to factories and shops, deeply conscious now of the ever-watchful eye that so soon became the over-vocal voice.

Time passed. Philip squired the sisters to dances. Though Margaret was still a schoolgirl, she now went about as freely as Lilibet.

Did Lilibet know what her parents thought of her love affair with Philip? I was never sure. That issue, like so many at the time, was a dark secret. A decision would eventually have to be taken, but meantime it was being pushed out of sight. Older members of the household, in touch with the King and Queen, were bothered about it.

'If there is not to be an engagement, the boy ought not to be around so much. There is too much talk and speculation already,' one of them said to me.

Margaret knew. There were no secrets between the sisters. Margaret came to my room one day, and fiddled around as she always did, picking up something and looking at it, and putting it down. Then she came and knelt down on the hearthrug beside me, and asked abruptly:

'Crawfie, do you like Philip?'

'Very much,' I said.

'But he's not English. Would it make a difference?'

'He's lived here all his life,' I told her. 'He's as English as you or I, really.'

For a long minute she said nothing at all. Then she said, very softly, 'Poor Lil. Nothing of your own. Not even your love affair!'

All this time Lilibet led a really remarkably quiet life com-pared with that of her sister Margaret today. She went to an occasional dance or play, squired by some young officer from the garrison, or by personal friends of the family. Looking back on it I am amazed to recall how very discreet and unspoiled she always was. The greater part of her day she gave up to performing what must often have been pretty dull duties, and this she did quite as a matter of course. Like her parents, she considered it her job, and it never struck her to try to avoid it.

She had very little social life of her own. On many occasions when I went to her room she would be gazing dreamily out of the window, no doubt worrying quite a bit in her own quiet way about the outcome of all this.

Lilibet has a large collection of snapshots, and the King and Queen never go anywhere without the movie camera. They took films of the babyhood of the Princesses, and have pictures right on up to date. They are often shown after tea at Royal Lodge, and much to our amusement the King would sometimes reverse the films so that we saw ourselves leaping out of the swimming pool back on to the board, or the horses or dogs going backwards.

One day I saw Lilibet had been busy with her photograph albums. When I looked to see what she had been doing, I noticed that she had stuck, for the first time, some snapshots of Philip among the family pictures.

When it was known that Prince Philip was going to Balmoral that autumn, public excitement and speculation brimmed over. The papers carried whole columns of 'inside information' and entirely unfounded stories. It must have been trying indeed for these two young people, between whom there had as yet been neither proposal nor acceptance.

The generally accepted idea was that this was for Prince Philip a trial trip. The King and Queen were commonly supposed to have invited Philip up to see whether he would be acceptable as a son-in-law.

The silliness of all this is apparent when it is realized that they had both known him from his boyhood, and had seen a great deal of him just previous to this in London. He was asked up because he was a young man they all liked, who would make an amusing addition to the party. Perhaps also to give Lilibet a good long spell of his company, to see how she liked him in large doses. Perhaps to give older members of the household an opportunity of getting to know him against the family background.

Nothing of that sort was said. But Lilibet was well aware that there were two schools of thought. Some of the King's advisers did not think him good enough for her. He was a prince without home or kingdom. Some of the papers played long and loud tunes on the string of Philip's foreign origin. There must have been for Lilibet in those autumn days, that should have been such happy ones for her, plenty of doubts, plenty of embarrassments, uncertainties, and heartaches. Her own mind never wavered for an instant. It was solidly made up.

It is good fun to be a princess in a palace. But not always. Not all the time. I have often thought how much, at Balmoral, Lilibet must have envied the Scottish lasses their peaceful courting at evening ends on moor and hillside.

My own view was that a young man who had served so long in the hard and severely disciplined Royal Navy, including active service, must have proved his manhood, and would be a worthy husband for any woman. Also, I knew that Philip was very well liked in the senior service by both officers and men – not because he was a prince, but for himself.

Philip's visit dragged on for more than a month. The young people went out with the guns and picnicked together, but they were very seldom alone. Occasionally he would take her out for a drive, and now and again they would manage to get off into the gardens after tea.

But the family is a very demanding one, and however

sympathetic the other guests might be, there was little they could do to help. The general feeling was that if nothing was to be announced, the boy ought to go south. It was fair to neither of them to keep him hanging around.

I was on my holidays at this time, but I heard all about it when I got back. The general opinion was that both Lilibet and Philip had had rather a bad break, and the summer could not have been much fun for them. Most of the household longed to see her happy in her own way, with a man of her own choice.

By this time we were all a little bewildered. I think what it really amounted to was that neither the King nor the Queen could make up their minds what was best for their very dear daughter, and so postponed decision. They wanted the best for her, and it is never easy for parents in any walk of life to decide what that best is.

Lilibet was quiet, her brightness suddenly shadowed. The royal discretion held even here, and she never discussed the problem with me. But I, who knew her well and loved her dearly, knew there would never be any other man for her.

The next move was an even more unlikely one. An official statement was issued from the Palace early in September, denying the rumour that there was an engagement between the two young people. On top of this came the announcement that Princess Elizabeth and her sister would accompany the King and Queen on their trip to South Africa early in 1947. Prince Philip, everyone noted, was not to be of the party.

It was a quiet and subdued little Princess who went about the task of collecting her frocks for the trip. She would be twenty-one in the spring of that year, but looked much younger. That unsophisticated air of hers has always been part of her charm. More than once, watching her, I was reminded of something I had read about Prince Albert, her great-great-grandfather, when he was a very young man:

'From the very first Prince Albert had shown a touching sweetness of disposition, a shy gentleness that was both moving and appealing.' Those words might have been written of Lilibet.

It was clear she was not happy about the South African trip. She would have liked to have matters fixed, and to be properly engaged before she went away, I know. Four months is a long, long time to a girl in love. Prince Philip was not in London at this time, but he rang her up every evening. She would grow restless as the hour they arranged came near. Then she would say to me, 'Someone is going to 'phone me, Crawfie. I must go.'

He came to the Palace still. Sometimes they would walk in the gardens together. Often he was one of a theatre or dancing party at which other young people, and usually Margaret, would also be present. They had very little time alone. I often felt that very few young people, in love as they two were, would have behaved with such self-control and discretion as they did at this time.

Prince Philip must have spoken of his feelings to the King and Queen, and no doubt they had told him that they felt it would be best if they did not see each other for a time. There was to be nothing definite arranged until after the South African visit.

Margaret's life held no complications. She was still only a schoolgirl, but was about to put her books away for a time and see the world, and she was wildly excited. She had never been out of the British Isles. There were new clothes to buy, a thing she always greatly enjoyed. Both Princesses got a coupon allocation for this trip, though it was by no means a lavish one.

This was the first occasion on which Margaret was given some real latitude in the choice of her outfit, and a very good use she made of it. The pink wool coat that was copied far and wide by teenagers of all classes was her own choice, as was the smart little hat with its two jaunty feathers.

Large wardrobes were essential on this trip because of the different climates they had to move in, one day cold, the next few days very hot. The official evening dresses they took with them were really beautiful. Picture frocks they were mostly, with wide skirts and the lovely embroideries at which Mr Hartnell excels. They also had two very snappy nautical outfits for wear on the *Vanguard*, with brass buttons and round sailor hats.

Out came the maps of Africa, and we went together over the whole ground they were to cover and read up on all the places they would visit. A special very beautiful train, called the White Train, was to be their headquarters while they were in Africa.

The Royal Family were to sail from Portsmouth on 1 February 1947. At one time there had been the idea I might accompany them, and I longed to go. My own romance, still postponed, depressed me, and I thought a change would be wonderful. No one quite knew until the last possible moment just who would be chosen to go, and there were many heart-searchings and false hopes.

Frenzied ladies-in-waiting often came to my room in those days to see if I knew any more of what was in Their Majesties' minds than they did.

'No one knows *what* to do, Crawfie. Whoever is finally chosen won't have time to get their clothes. The King and Queen don't realize how difficult it is.'

Dressmakers in those days were harried, short-handed, coupon-conscious, and difficult. The ladies-in-waiting finally chosen to go had great difficulty in getting their clothes together, just as they feared. They needed considerable wardrobes because of the variety of climates.

The King and Queen, about a month before they left, came

up to the schoolroom and we discussed various matters to do with Margaret, and both said they had been very pleased with the progress she had made.

'I think we both realize that this break in routine is perhaps a pity,' said the Queen, 'but it seemed too bad to separate the family just now.'

This was the first and only intimation I ever had that Their Majesties had faced the fact that a final break was coming.

'At one time we thought of taking you with us, Crawfie. But Margaret would have scant time for lessons, and we have decided you must have a well-earned rest while we are away.'

'Do you think, ma'am,' I asked, 'that perhaps the time has come to make a break altogether? Margaret is growing up. On her return from this trip I do not feel she will take to schoolroom routine very easily again.'

'Crawfie, don't suggest such a thing! Of course she must go back to her lessons.' The Queen looked horrified.

I thought Her Majesty did not relish the thought of having to deal alone with what might prove to be a spoiled and disorganized young girl when the party got back. I believe at that time I did not entirely relish the prospect myself. Margaret had always had so much more of her own way, and so much more freedom than her sister. In my own mind I had come to the conclusion that this very grown-up trip would be the last straw. She was always wilful and headstrong. *When she comes back after all this*, I thought, *she will not settle down*.

I was wrong. Margaret's character is like a well-cut diamond. It has facets in every direction which reflect all kinds of light.

Everyone assembles in the Bow Room in the Palace when the family is going on a journey. Relations see them off from railway station or quayside.

The Bow Room is a very large State apartment on the

ground floor. It has a big bow window that gives on to wide steps leading to the gardens. It was remodelled in 1844 and is done up now in red and gold.

The King and Queen came in, wearing their travelling clothes. The King had on his naval uniform and looked, I thought then, desperately tired. The Queen looked very sweet and pretty in her favourite blue. Lilibet was sad and we all thought that she did not want very much to go. Margaret, very grown up in her pink coat and gay hat with its little feathers, hugged me hard.

'Write often, Crawfie,' she said. 'We look to you for news of the dogs and horses.'

At the doorway she turned again for a moment and gave me a little look and a wave. I was very surprised to see there were tears in her eyes.

How empty and still it was when the cheers from the waiting crowds outside the Palace gates had died away and they were gone!

I have wondered since whether the King and Queen thought that maybe a trip abroad, and the new sights and adventures to be found there, would make Lilibet forget what was, after all, her first love affair. She was so very young. Other parents have staked everything on the foreign journey and the long separation, often with some measure of success. They had nothing against Philip; indeed, they had always liked him. But they wanted her to be quite sure.

There never had been any doubt in my mind. I knew she would not change. Where Lilibet gives her love and affection, she gives it once and for all.

She wrote him constantly. Her letters were sent back to him in the royal mailbag. No obstacles were ever put in her way. She had Philip's photograph with her on her dressing-table or bureau throughout the whole trip. When her lady-in-waiting asked her once whether or not there was any truth in the stories that went around of a probable engagement, Lilibet told her to 'wait and see'.

A picture of them all on the *Vanguard* leaving England on 1 February shows the King and Queen looking pleased at the prospect of two weeks' rest at sea. Margaret, obviously very gay and excited, is beside them. Lilibet is standing at the ship's rail looking back sadly towards England.

About three weeks after they had left, there descended on England a winter we shall none of us forget. Everything froze. Temperatures were lower than in the memory of any living man. Roads became impassable with snow, and later ice-bound. Plumbing went out of action for weeks on end; water-sources froze solid. To increase the general misery the fuel crisis, when the coal supply gave out, cut down still further our chances of keeping warm, or even for long spells every day doing any cooking. The wireless would issue its hateful message every morning, 'There will be a fuel cut between the hours of – and – ,' after which all current would be cut off.

I remember writing to Margaret and telling her I had cut my face on an icicle which had formed on my sheet in bed from my own breath. Food, never good since the war, became alarmingly worse. The cold weather stopped hens laying, food ships were held up in dock, and lorries could not get along roads. The country shops emptied because no one could get supplies to them. Trains did not run, or took several days on the way. In the worst of the blitz we had never had to endure anything like the discomfort and cold of those February and March days.

I was in Scotland at this time. Here things were even worse than in England. I wanted to go to Edinburgh to do some shopping. The journey normally took three-quarters of an hour. But on this day the points on the railway had frozen, and

The South African tour of 1947. The Royal Family greet members of the Indian community at Pietermaritzburg, Natal

On the steps of Government House, Salisbury. Princess Elizabeth has just been presented with a diamond brooch subscribed to by 42,000 Rhodesian school-children. Standing with her is the deputation of children who presented the gift

The Princesses inspect the diamonds presented to them at Kimberley

The Royal Family go for a stroll with Field-Marshal Smuts during a restful three days spent at the Natal National Park

Prince Philip with the Princesses at Buckingham Palace

*The engagement picture. After the official announcement, Princess
Elizabeth chats happily with her fiancé and proudly displays her new ring*

The wedding ceremony at Westminster Abbey, 20 November 1947

After the service the smiling bride leaves the Abbey on the arm of her husband

The wedding group. The best man stands on the Throne Room dais with the bride and groom. With the King and Queen is the Dowager Countess of Milford Haven. Princess Andrew of Greece stands with Queen Mary

The best man and bridesmaids join the crowd in the Palace courtyard to give the honeymooners a royal send-off

The happy couple wave to the crowd as they drive from Buckingham Palace to Waterloo Station, where a special train waits to take them to Winchester, on their way to Broadlands, Earl Mountbatten's Hampshire home

Marion Crawford at the gate of Nottingham Cottage

Opposite: *A honeymoon photograph*

Princess Margaret, visiting the Port of London Authority, walks through the street from Trinity House to Tower Pier. She is accompanied by Sir John Anderson, Chairman of the PLA

After officially naming the London Missionary Society's new ship, the John Williams VI, *Princess Margaret speaks from the bridge*

*The Queen and Princess Margaret chat with Don Bradman at Balmoral Castle,
where they entertained the members of the Australian cricket team to tea*

*At the Royal Windsor Horse Show Princess Margaret presents a prize to the
winner of the Children's Jumping Competition*

Princess Margaret, President of Dr Barnardo's Homes, photographed with some of the children in the garden of St Christopher's home at Tunbridge Wells

Princess Margaret attends a charity ball. On her right is the Marquess of Blandford

Princess Elizabeth presents a trophy to the winner of the Diamond Sculls at Henley Regatta

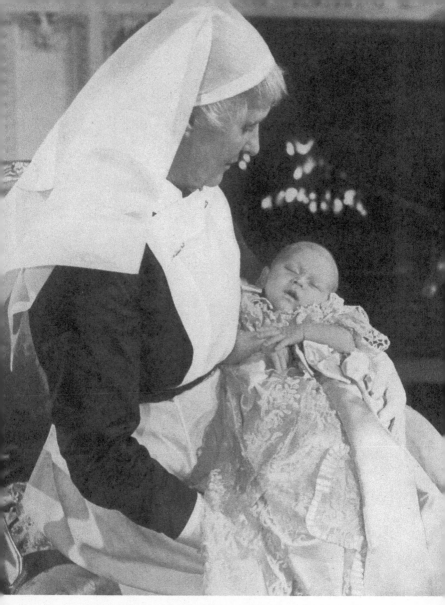

The infant Prince Charles in the arms of his nurse after his christening at Buckingham Palace

Playtime for Princess Elizabeth and her son and heir

A portrait of Princess Margaret

the train stood on the Forth Bridge for two hours, unable to move. Down below, the Forth looked extremely uninviting, with ice forming on the water. The skies hung over us like a chill grey tent, and one got to the pitch of almost feeling the thaw would never come and the Ice Age had begun.

I kept my promise and wrote regularly and fully to the Princesses. I gave them accounts of our somewhat macabre existence and the life we were leading. I sent them copies of the Aberdeen papers with pictures of sheep frozen stiff in the fields close to Birkhall.

The letters I got back were a great pleasure to me. They were also a wonderful picture of the different make-up of the two sisters. Margaret wrote with her usual gaiety, all about the fun they were having, how beautiful the White Train was, how warm the sun, how wonderful the food.

Lilibet wrote, immensely distressed by all that was going on in England in the bitter weather. It bothered her to feel she was far away having a good time, in a land so full of everything. She felt she ought to be at home.

They sent me copies of the *Cape Town Argus* every day while they were away, so I was able to keep in touch with their doings.

It was while the family were away on the South African trip that my own affairs once again filled my horizon, and I decided that the time had come when I could, in all fairness to the King and Queen, and the Princesses, arrange for my own marriage to take place as soon as the Royal Family returned from South Africa.

I did not quite know how I was to break this news to the King and Queen, who, I was well aware, relied on me to take charge of Margaret on their return.

I determined to confide in Queen Mary and to ask her

advice. So I wrote to her, and the day before the family were to get back I went to tea at Marlborough House. I was shown into the garden with its neat lawn and pretty, well-kept flower beds. I made my deep curtsy and kissed the Queen's hand. She then raised me, and kissed me on both cheeks.

'Come now, Crawfie, sit down and tell me all about it,' said Queen Mary in her kind way, meantime spearing for me a muffin on a small silver fork. Her Majesty never touches any food with her fingers.

I told her I was very well, and that I had come to ask her advice, as I wanted to get married. Queen Mary's first reaction was a typical one.

'My dear child. You can't leave them!' she said, shocked.

I then told her the whole story, how I had shelved the matter during the war years, feeling it was my duty then to stay. But I said surely the time had come when I might look for a life of my own.

'Princess Margaret is growing up very fast now,' I pointed out, 'and I think we all know in our own minds that it will not be very long before Princess Elizabeth marries.'

'You think so? You think Lilibet will marry him? I know nothing. No one has told me. He seems a good boy, I think. Tell me, Crawfie, you who know her so well, would it be a success?'

I told her I thought they were very deeply in love, and that for the Princess there would never be any other man for whom she would feel the same.

The old Queen sighed. 'Well. We must wait and see, and hope for the best,' she said. She had lost her own eldest son through a love affair, and I think perhaps it had disillusioned her a little with romances of any kind. Later she was to become very fond of Philip.

As to my personal problem, Her Majesty advised me to speak to the Queen when the Royal Family got back, and see what her reactions were.

'But,' added Queen Mary, 'I don't see how they could manage without you. I don't think they could spare you just now.'

There is no doubt whatever that the African trip was a very great strain on the whole family. For Lilibet it had been a long and anxious separation from the man she loved. It was four months since she had seen Philip. For the King and Queen it meant a great deal of journeying and exhausting work coming on top of the strain of the war years, and for Margaret it was a trip I considered her neither old enough nor strong enough to undertake at that time. It had been too much for all of them.

I shall never forget the shock I had when we all assembled at Buckingham Palace again to welcome them on their return. It was an exciting moment, watching them get out of the cars. We were all in the Grand Hall to meet them. I had their pet dogs, who, after the manner of dogs, seemed to have sensed early that morning that something was up.

I was horrified to see how thin Lilibet had gone. She had also lost all her pretty colour and looked pale and drawn. But she of all of them had a sort of inner radiance, doubtless for reasons of her own. The lady-in-waiting told me that as the *Vanguard* steamed into harbour she had danced a little jig of sheer delight at being home again.

The King and Queen looked positively worn out. I thought at first the King's hair had gone quite grey in his four months' absence. Later I saw it was just bleached by the hot sun. Margaret looked ill and tired out. She looked the worst of them all, and I was secretly very anxious about her.

How gay they all were, and how happy to be back. The two Princesses hugged me and kissed me, and everyone seemed to be talking at once. There was so much to tell, so many things to show me. The diamond companies of South Africa had given both the Princesses some very fine diamonds, and Margaret had already made little sketches of

how hers would be made up and what she would do with the
two large diamonds left over from the bracelet which was too
big for her.

There was a pile of letters waiting for Lilibet, and she soon
went off to her own room to read them and, I've no doubt, to
telephone to Philip. He did not appear at all at the return
celebrations. But later he came to dinner. His small sports car
was again to be seen constantly at the side entrance. The old
routine began. Surely, we all thought, something *must* be
arranged now.

It was not only on Lilibet's account that I felt in those days
worked up and excited. I had my own problem. Presently I
sent a note along to the Queen asking her if she would see me
on a very urgent and important matter of a personal nature.

I went to Her Majesty's sitting room with a photograph
of my husband-to-be under my arm. I made my usual deep
curtsy, and then presented the photograph to the Queen.

'This, ma'am,' I said, 'is the urgent personal matter I have
come to see you about.'

The Queen took the photograph from me. She was obviously very surprised and somewhat disconcerted. She asked
me his name, and I told her that it was George Buthlay and
that he came from Aberdeen.

She stood for a long time saying nothing whatever. I broke
this uncomfortable silence presently and told her how at the
start of the war I had wanted very much to marry, and had not
done so because I felt I had a duty to Their Majesties, and
considered it would be unfair of me to leave the Princesses
when they most needed me. But now, I said, the time had
come when I wanted a life of my own.

The Queen said gently, 'Why, Crawfie, that was a great
sacrifice you made.'

'Does this mean you are going to leave us?' she asked me.
'You must see, Crawfie, that it would not be at all convenient

just now. A change at this stage for Margaret is not at all desirable.'

I assured the Queen the last thing George and I wanted to do was upset Their Majesties' plans in any way, and that for the time being I would be prepared to carry on with my work and live at the Palace for as long as they wished me to, even after I was married.

'After all, ma'am, it will not be for so very much longer that I shall be required here,' I said. I waited, hoping perhaps the Queen would confide in me then what their intentions were for Lilibet, but she said nothing further, and I curtsied and withdrew.

I had expected to get Margaret back a very cross, spoiled, and disorganized young person after all her travels and the compliments and grown-up treatment she had had, which had been more than sufficient to turn the head of any teenage girl.

I was entirely wrong. She was as good as gold. I really think she was quite glad to get back to her peaceful schoolroom life, for a little while, anyway. She arrived for lessons wearing as usual a very simple wool frock, carrying the same pencil-box she had used as a small child. It was always full of very small pencils pared right down to the stub. This was a form of economy both the girls practised, which had always amused me a lot. They used their erasers in the same way, down to the last rub. Obediently, Margaret settled down to her books again, for all the world as if she had never been away.

I now concentrated on getting her finished. We did a lot of history and literature and general reading, and concentrated more than before on poetry and modern plays. At one time I tried to arrange for Margaret to go to Sir Henry Marten for advanced history, as her sister had done. Nothing came of this scheme, however. For one thing, Sir Henry was far from well.

For another, Margaret's social life became more and more demanding.

At last things were moving. Suddenly that look of strain we had all been conscious of disappeared from Lilibet's eyes. One day she poked her head into my room looking absolutely radiant.

'Crawfie,' she said, 'something is going to happen at last!'

'It's about time,' was all I could say, and there was a big lump in my throat.

'He's coming tonight,' she said, and then she kissed me and danced away.

Next morning was Wednesday, 9 July. Lilibet came to my room much earlier than usual. I have never seen her look lovelier than she did on that day, not even on her wedding morning. She wore a deep yellow frock, a shade that has always suited her very well. She closed the door behind her and held out her left hand.

Her engagement ring sparkled there. It was a large square diamond with smaller diamonds either side. At that time it was too large for her, and it had to go back to be made smaller. It was a ring they had chosen together secretly, but of course she had been unable to go and try it on.

That was a happy day for all of us. The morning papers announced in a Court Circular that the King had been graciously pleased to give his assent to the betrothal of his beloved daughter to Lieutenant Philip Mountbatten. Philip's naturalization papers had come through, and he had dropped his title of Prince. He was a junior officer now in the Royal Navy, and had taken the family name of his uncle, Lord Louis Mountbatten, who had been his guardian most of his life and had given him the only home he had ever known.

The romance did something wonderful to the Palace. All of a sudden the gloomy corridors seemed lighter. Everyone was immensely excited and pleased, for the tall, rather unconventional young man who had been around for some time had made many friends for himself. He appeared presently, looking very handsome and happy. I congratulated him and said how very glad I was that everything had come right for them at last.

He looked down at me and smiled. 'I'm so proud of her, Crawfie.'

'Sir, you have good reason to be. And who should know that better than I?' I replied.

Photographers as usual filled the horizon for a while. All question of lessons was shelved for the next few days. Margaret was sweet, happy in her sister's happiness as if it had been her own. She was growing out of her one-time objection to Lilibet's doing anything she could not do, or having a train longer than hers. The air was full of wedding talk and planning, which for me had a personal note.

CHAPTER XI

The Royal Wedding

I had now decided my own marriage should take place quietly during my next trip to Scotland. I said nothing to the King or Queen about this. It seemed to me they had already enough on their hands. Both George and I had already decided we wished to be married without any fuss.

Some weeks later, in September, the Queen was at Holyrood House in Scotland with Margaret, and I was at home in Dunfermline on my usual holiday. She telegraphed me to come to tea with her. I went wearing my engagement ring for the first time. This brought the subject up at once. It was no longer possible to ignore it or shelve the problem, or push it away in the background for that future consideration which so often never took place.

No one could have been kinder than Her Majesty. The Queen kissed me and wished me great happiness, but added, 'I do hope you won't think of leaving us just yet. It is going to be such a busy time.'

Once again I made my promise that I would remain as long as I was needed, though I realized this meant postponing still further the real start of my married life or making a home of my own.

We then had tea. Later Margaret flung her arms around my neck and said, 'I am so glad that you are going to stay near me, Crawfie.'

When Ainslie, handsome and correct as ever, came in with the tea, the Queen said to him, 'What do you think, Ainslie? Miss Crawford is also going to be married.'

Ainslie congratulated me in his courtly way. I have often thought what a wonderful Archbishop of Canterbury he would have made had he applied his talents in other directions. He departed. When I went out to go home I found he had collected all his staff in the hall, where they stood lined up to congratulate me in their turn before I left.

George and I were married very quietly on 16 September 1947, by the Reverend Robert Dollar, BD, in Dunfermline Abbey. I had congratulatory messages and telegrams from all the Royal Family and later several wedding presents arrived. Queen Mary sent me a complete and very beautiful dinner service, the Princess Royal gave me a visitors' book. Princess Margaret three bedside lamps, and Lilibet a coffee set.

Margaret now came to the front much more. As soon as Lilibet was married she would take her place as the Princess in the Palace. Among her first grown-up duties was the launching of a ship, all on her own. She went to Ireland alone, except for a lady-in-waiting to look after her. One charming incident there was peculiarly Margaret. She was presented with a bouquet of red roses by a hot and blushing young sailor. And she smiled at him in a way that I am sure must have made his heart beat faster, and pulled a rose from her bouquet and gave it to him for his own.

It was the sort of endearing human thing that my little Duchess would have done years back when I first knew her. So many of Margaret's more charming ways are inherited from her mother.

This Ireland trip came as a blessing to George and me, still on our honeymoon in Scotland. It gave us a few more days

together. Then I had to return south. We had a rather sad little
farewell as I left on the night train. We did not know how long
our separation was to be.

I arrived back at the Palace to find Lilibet's wedding preparations under way. The place seemed to be knee-deep in
tissue-paper. Mr Hartnell and his ladies were for ever trooping
up the stairs or hurrying down them, or waiting about discon-
solately, in ante-room or passage, where Bobo sometimes
revived them with cups of tea.

They who minister to royalty do a lot of waiting about. I
often wondered what the rest of Mr Hartnell's clientele did in
those days of the autumn collection.

Lilibet was very happy now, and happiness, as it so often
does, had transfigured her. She was sweet and thoughtful
of me, happy and thrilled that I had got married first. I
remember how she came laughing into my room one day and
I showed her an American paper someone had sent me.
GOVERNESS BEATS LIZ TO THE ALTAR, said the headlines.

We got a lot of amusement out of that. No one has ever
given the Princess that particular nickname, as it happens,
although Margaret sometimes in the bosom of the family has
called her Lil.

Lilibet was immensely touched by the way her romance
seemed to appeal to the world in general. Letters and telegrams
came from every kind of place and person. Girls wrote her that
they planned to marry on the same day. Sailors who had served
with Philip wrote her from ships at sea. She would bring a sheaf
of these messages to show me, touched almost to tears. I think
it was the first time she realized how many people loved her
who had never seen her, and just what it was she stood for.

Wedding presents poured in. One day Lilibet asked me,
'Crawfie, what have you done with George all this time?'

I told her George was in Scotland still, unable to make any
plans until we knew what was to happen to me.

'But Crawfie, he must come to my wedding,' Lilibet said, and promptly saw to it that George had an invitation. So he came south. We could meet but little in those busy days, but occasionally he came to the Palace to see me.

Princess Elizabeth asked me to bring George to my rooms at the Palace, in order that she and Princess Margaret should meet him. As soon as they were introduced, Lilibet said, 'I hope you are going to keep Crawfie in order, because she has certainly bullied us for the last sixteen years!'

George said we all three talked the same way, and laughed and moved our hands the same way. He was so struck by the charm of the two Princesses and how pleasant and easy they were, and, like everyone else, he spoke especially of the beauty of Lilibet's face and the charming vivacity and quick wit of Margaret.

He came again, I remember, the night before the wedding. We heard the most awful sounds coming from the old music room. They were all trying to sing Crimond's 'The Lord's My Shepherd,' because Lilibet wanted it at her wedding. They could not get the descant right, and they were humming it to Doctor McKee, organist of Westminster Abbey, who had come in.

We were swamped with wedding presents, and everything else was forgotten meantime. Margaret behaved to all intents and purposes like a grown-up young lady, and both her parents encouraged her. She was a real help and pleasure to them.

Philip was now a constant visitor. He and Lilibet would be together in the sitting room, which I noticed he had improved a lot. Philip has strong ideas about furnishing. Soon after the courtship started I saw that a large sofa was drawn in front of the fire with the chairs on either side, instead of being isolated in the window, with two solitary chairs on the hearthrug. So already he had begun to have his influence, and instead of looking stiff and unlived in, as I had often thought that sitting room did, it now had a homelike look.

The wedding day was fixed. I always felt myself that both the King and Queen would have preferred it to be put off until the spring or early summer when the weather was pleasant, and the reception could have been held in the gardens of the Palace. But the young couple felt they had waited long enough. Like other young people, on this subject they had their own ideas.

I did not bother Margaret with lessons. She had enough on hand. Nor did I feel that physically she had entirely recovered from the African tour. She still tired easily and refused to own when she was tired. I knew that once all the excitement had died down, we would make up for lost time.

The people of Wales sent a piece of Welsh gold for the wedding ring. This is a metal found only in very small quantities in Wales. It looks the same as any other yellow gold. The royal wedding rings are always made of it. Lilibet was particularly pleased when the piece that was to make her own ring arrived, and in that delightful way she had of always wanting to see Margaret wasn't left out, she told me:

'There is enough for two rings. We can save a piece for Margaret.'

They would walk about the gardens together, the two of them, Lilibet in her corn-coloured wool dress, Philip very tall and slender, his arm through hers, his lint-fair head bent towards her. I could see them from my window, and I thought what a handsome couple they made.

I also thought it was probably a long time since anyone wore quite such unconventional garments around the Palace. Philip's favourite kit was flannel trousers (not always very new or creased) and a tennis shirt with open neck, and often rolled-up sleeves. Hatless he would arrive, driving his own small sports car, always in a hurry to see Lilibet. Driving his own small sports car a great deal too fast!

Late one night after he had gone the telephone rang. A scared equerry came to inform the King that Lieutenant Mountbatten, on his way home, had skidded and overturned his car in a ditch. Lilibet had to be told. She was very upset and anxious, and insisted she speak to him on the telephone herself. I think she knew he was not the world's most cautious driver. Beyond a shaking, he was none the worse and apparently no more cautious.

Certain officials of the household, all of whom were devoted to Lilibet and had been her slaves since childhood, were greatly perturbed about this. They did not feel that Philip should be allowed to drive the heir to the throne about London as he had been doing.

It was surprising to all of us that the King did not forbid him, but I have no doubt whatever that Philip was gravely cautioned by His Majesty. I know the Queen must have been very worried, because when the children were small she was for ever saying to the King (not by any means a rash driver), 'Darling, *do not go so fast!*'

Another side to the problem was the general reluctance of the Palace chauffeurs to have Philip take out any of their beautifully kept cars, which might be returned to them with unsightly dents and buckled fenders.

There was another unfortunate incident not long afterwards when once again Philip was driving, and at Hyde Park Corner they had a slight mix-up with a taxicab. Lilibet came running in to me when they got home, very bothered.

'Oh, Crawfie, how am I to make Mummie and Papa realize that this time it *really* wasn't Philip's fault,' she said. 'It was the taxi. They will never believe it.'

❄

I saw the sketches of Lilibet's final choice of a wedding dress and patterns of the lovely material it was to be fashioned of as soon as Lilibet had made up her mind. I felt a very special interest in it, because the material finally chosen was woven and spun in my own home town, Dunfermline. There is a Swiss factory there that spins the particular weight Mr Hartnell needed for his wonderful embroidery design. It had to be very strong, yet not heavy.

There was resentment in some quarters about the secrecy that was maintained over the wedding gown and the brides- maids' frocks. But I felt that in all Lilibet's romance she had been able to keep so little to herself and had been so dogged and hampered by rumour and speculation that it gave her pleasure to feel that she had something entirely private and all her own. Princesses like to forget, sometimes, how little they belong to themselves. Everything else to do with the wedding had been written about in the papers. Some of the accounts were quite fantastic flights of fancy. Every aspect of the young people's future had been commented on and explored. There was no feeling at all for a young and sensitive girl, and what her reaction would be to public speculation on the number of children she might have, and what their rank would be.

Royalty earn every penny they get, for their loss of privacy at times like this.

Parcels began to pour in, hundreds of them, from all parts of the world. The contents of some of them were quite amazing. One evening the lady-in-waiting and I started after dinner to open some of them. The old schoolroom was by this time full of every kind of oddment. The Keeper of the King's Pictures had brought up a number of them for Lilibet to choose from, and so parcels were stacked in the lady-in-waiting's room, which soon looked like a depository in a railway station.

I always loved opening parcels, even if they were not for me. I picked one up, cut the string, removed several layers of paper, and found two soggy masses in my hand. I flung them away in horror. It was two slices of very burned and damp toast. With them came a letter from two young women who had been making toast when they heard the news of the Princess's engagement on the wireless. They were so excited and thrilled they burned their toast to a cinder, so sent the very toast to the Princess with a charming little letter of congratulation. How we laughed!

Another parcel that fell to me to open was very securely tied up with layer upon layer of stout paper.

'Whatever have you got there?' asked the lady-in-waiting.

'Something round and very heavy,' I told her facetiously. 'It's probably a bomb!'

I quickly snatched off the last piece of paper, holding the thing at arm's length. It was a large, rugged piece of rock. An old man from Wales had sent it for luck. It was, he said, a piece of Snowdon.

An old lady sent a lace underslip, beautiful hand-done Victorian work. It had been worn by the brides of her family for generations.

For the first time, an old-established convention was broken. Lilibet was allowed to keep presents that were sent her. At other royal weddings, presents were accepted only from persons the family knew. It would have been difficult to return gifts that were sent with such deep love and loyalty, but I often felt some of the priceless heirlooms that came should have remained in the families to which they really belonged.

The letters were wonderfully touching. The Princess herself read every one of these. A lot of people sent their clothing coupons to help her with her trousseau, but these were always returned by registered post, with a letter of thanks from the Princess. It was not legal to give clothing coupons away.

Hundreds of beautiful handkerchiefs, linen, lace, and the sheerest lawn were sent to her. There were hundreds of pairs of nylon stockings. Gloomy old Buckingham Palace suddenly took on the appearance of a treasure-house.

The magnitude of it all bewildered Lilibet. She was, in those days, rushed off her feet and hardly knew where she was. She had been so very simply brought up. Until quite recently her idea of a nice birthday or Christmas present had been a Victorian posy, a china ornament, or a needle-book fashioned, with grief and pain, by her own hand. After the scarcity, the make-do of the war years, this sudden lavishness and plenty was unnerving. I often thought it bothered Lilibet a little, in those days of austerity, to have so much when many had so little. She was always a thoughtful young person.

She had, like all other brides, a small extra allotment of coupons given to her by the Board of Trade, for her trousseau. But there was, besides, a great deal of material at the Palace bought at different times and places by the Queen, and Queen Mary, to say nothing of gifts of silk and muslin, and brocades that came from distant parts of the Empire. All this helped with the trousseau.

The wedding presents were displayed in St James's Palace, which came to resemble an Ali Baba's cave of treasure – and horrors! People paid a shilling for admittance after the first day, when I believe it was five shillings. A very large sum was raised for charity in this manner. After the wedding the beautiful wedding dress was on view here too.

The crowds waiting to get in and have a look often would stretch for a mile along the Mall. We could see them waiting there from the Palace windows.

Lilibet said, 'I have so much! Crawfie, you are getting a home together also. You must share some of all this with me. Make out a list of the things you will be needing most.'

I had great fun compiling the list, for in the midst of all this plenty, curtains for my own little home had presented a real problem. The King had given me for my life-time one of the

Grace and Favour houses which are in His Majesty's personal gift. This one was attached to Kensington Palace, looking over the Palace Green. It is a small cottage, designed by Christopher Wren. It looks as if it had got to London quite by mistake from some distant country place. It is built of lovely seasoned red brick, with a tiled roof and roses round the door. It has a little square garden behind a low white paling, where snapdragons, and lavender, and scented white Mrs Simpkins border carnations grow. I had never before had a home of my own, and to me it seemed wonderful. Like a dream at last come true. I used to stand back to admire the name painted on the little white gate, NOTTINGHAM COTTAGE. Queen Mary knew the place well, as she had been born in Kensington Palace and in other days had often been to have tea in the cottage. Sometimes a flock of sheep are put to graze in the field over the way, and at evening the lamplighter trudges round still lighting up the old-fashioned gas-lamps. The roar of the traffic in Kensington High Street sounds thin and far-off and in springtime the voices of the birds drown it altogether.

Margaret was almost as intrigued by my little house as I myself was. She frequently came down there with me to help me plan and choose my colour schemes, and made many a useful suggestion. I could not help thinking, as she sang about the little rooms, what a wonderful housewife she herself would make, and how well she would run her home, and how elegant and pretty she would make it look.

But I had my problems. Curtain materials and coverings for floors and furniture were not only in short supply, they were a truly terrible price.

These, together with various other matters, had to be shelved for the time being. I had too much to do to bother about my own affairs. The wedding day was upon us. From the Palace windows the whole world seemed a-flutter with flags. The crowds had begun to gather the night before, and by daylight the whole Mall was a solid mass of people, with mounted police riding up and down on their splendid horses, keeping the main road clear. Great numbers had slept out, and were having picnic breakfasts, and cooking bacon over little stoves. It was funny to open the window and find, with the usual roaring noise, the smell of coffee drifting in.

There had been no last-minute festivities inside the Palace, no evening party or gathering of any kind. There was too much to do. The King and Queen and their daughters dined quietly together. After that there was a mass of detail to be gone into for tomorrow's function. Gold chairs were stacked up in the banqueting rooms. The whole air smelt of flowers.

Lilibet went to bed very early. Philip had looked in during the evening and said his last good night to her. She came up to her room, singing. There was a lovely feeling in the Palace that night. We were all of us happy because she was happy, and things had at last gone right for her.

I don't think any of us had very much sleep. I went along to Lilibet's room very early, and found her in her dressing-gown, peeping excitedly out of the windows at the crowds.

'I can't believe it's really happening, Crawfie,' she said. 'I have to keep pinching myself.'

She had been down as usual for the session with Papa and Mummie in their room. They must all have been a little sad that morning, as people are when it comes to last times. Standing there, peeping through the curtain, she looked such a child still, it was difficult to realize she was grown up, and would today be a bride. I stood in the doorway for a moment, looking back at her, and I could not help remembering that small golden-headed little girl I had first seen – could it *really* be sixteen years ago? – sitting up in bed, the cord of her dressing-gown tied to the bedposts, driving her imaginary team round the park. I thought of Alah, and how dearly she would have loved this day, with her darling decked out in splendour, and surrounded with all the magnificence and ceremony Alah always felt to be a princess's due.

Of course there were the usual last-minute crises, the tensions common to any home on a wedding morning. The bouquet got lost. A footman remembered receiving it and bringing it upstairs, but what happened to it after that nobody could imagine. It had gone! When the uproar was at its height, the footman suddenly remembered he had bethought of himself to put it into a cupboard to keep cool.

Then Lilibet decided she must wear a certain wedding-present string of pearls, and she sent for them, only to be told they could not be found either. After much agitation, someone remembered they had been sent over with the rest of the wedding presents to St James's Palace, and were on view there.

Her private secretary, Mr John Colville, volunteered to go over and fetch them for her. He departed at the double. Unfortunately, the detectives on duty at St James's did not know Mr Colville. They listened to his story and thought it extremely fishy. They were taking no risks. In vain he pleaded with them; they refused to let him have the pearls. In the end, he was allowed to take them back to the Palace with a police-man and a couple of detectives accompanying him, ready to pounce should he show any tendency to melt into the crowds!

The only person who remained throughout calm and cool was the staunch Bobo. She dressed her Princess, and then went over to the Abbey to be on hand to take care of her when she arrived there.

The Queen looked beautiful that day. She wore a dress of apricot-coloured silk brocade, which I thought immensely more becoming to her than her usual shades of pastel violet, blue, or mauve. The dress was plainly and simply cut, and with it went an apricot-coloured hat, and wonderful jewels that caught the light in a thousand different colours as she moved. Her face was the face of my little Duchess painted by Sorin long ago.

She must have remembered another great occasion when she, a girl herself, had driven through just such crowds and rejoicings, to marry the man she loved. Through the years I had had many reasons for admiring the Queen's self-control, but I never admired it more than on that, her elder daughter's wedding morning. And I thought, as I watched her enter the Abbey and kneel for a moment in prayer, that the most she could ask for her child was the happiness she herself had found in her own marriage.

Lilibet had arranged seats for George and myself in Poets' Corner, not far from the King and Queen. 'You must be near us,' she said, 'as you have been all these years.'

There is always a nerve-racking moment, waiting for the bride to appear. It had been a dull morning, but now for a few moments a thin, watery sun shone through the stained-glass windows, lighting the feathers and silks and jewels of the waiting guests. I remember feeling rather sick, just as I did on our pantomime mornings, or before a State ball. The bells that hold such heart-rending memories for all of us clashed out overhead, and every time the doors opened to admit anyone we heard far off that curious murmur that is the voice of a crowd. The organ played softly. We were all of us on tenterhooks, lest something had gone wrong since we left the Palace. I know I saw the Queen give a little sigh of relief when at last the great doors were thrown open and the Princess came.

A princess she looked, that morning. She was pale. She had used hardly any make-up. Her veil was a white cloud about her, and light from the tall windows and from the candelabra caught and reflected the jewelled embroidery of her frock. Her long spreading train (held with determination by Prince William and Prince Michael in dress kilts and silk shirts), her wide skirts and billowing veil made her seem suddenly much taller than she really was.

One can never tell how young pages will behave on these awesome occasions, but both Prince William and Prince Michael played their parts admirably. The former had one unrehearsed moment, however, when he tripped over part of the lighting or loud-speaking apparatus and would have fallen but for the prompt action of the quick-witted Princess Margaret, who deftly caught him in time. It was so neatly done that few noticed the incident.

If Lilibet was nervous, she did not show it as she came slowly down the aisle on her father's arm. The King wore the uniform that becomes him best, that of Admiral of the Fleet. Directly behind her sister, three paces ahead of the other bridesmaids, in emphasis of her rank, came Margaret, alone.

I hope people were not too taken up with the bride that day to notice her younger sister. The full-skirted net frock Margaret wore made her, too, look taller. She moved with extraordinary dignity and grace, her head held high. More than once the King and Queen exchanged a smile and a re-assuring glance.

The service must have been a poignant one for the Queen, with its many memories. The past must have gone through her mind, as it went through mine, in a series of pictures of what had been an unusually happy family circle. A home in which no doors banged, and voices were never raised in anger, and a little girl had grown to womanhood with natural good manners and a charm peculiarly her own. If the years had not brought them quite what they had expected, there was so much to be glad of and proud about.

Lilibet herself had chosen all the hymns and the tunes to be played during the service, and one she chose in the old Scottish paraphrase that we of the north love so much because it is a part of our childhood. It was sung to the tune of Crimond:

> The Lord's my shepherd, I'll not want.
> He makes me down to lie
> In pastures green: he leadeth me
> the quiet waters by.

And then it was over, and Lilibet came out of the vestry on her tall husband's arm, with that radiant look on her face all brides should have. And when she came to the place where her father and mother, the King and Queen, stood, she paused for a moment and swept them a beautiful curtsy. To many of us there, this was the most touching and poignant moment of the service.

There is nothing in the world so attractive as gentleness and good manners. I have often thought that the young people who copy the Princesses' hats and frocks, and shoes, and ways of dressing, would do well also to copy their beautiful manners. To me, gentleness and lovely manners are far more important than clothes. For good manners are a charm that never goes out of fashion, and requires no capital outlay.

> God gave to mankind graces three
> The best of these is courtesie.

To the wild pealing of the bells, and the cheers of the crowds clustering about the Abbey, we waited for our cars. I had been invited to the family lunch party at Buckingham Palace, and for a while it looked as if I would never get there. In the end my husband managed to get a police car to give me a lift. I arrived at the Privy Purse door with just three minutes to spare, and no time to tidy myself or powder my nose. I had a cherry-red velvet frock, and a large black hat with black ostrich feathers held in place with ruby clips.

It was a gay and merry lunch party. The tables were decorated with smilax and white carnations, and at each of our places there was a little bunch of white heather, sent down from Balmoral. The famous gold plate and the scarlet-coated footmen gave a fairy-tale atmosphere to it all, and I was in a veritable dream. The skirl of the bagpipes warmed the hearts of those of us who came from north of the Tweed. The French gentleman seated next to me, however, winced from time to time, but he bore it with fortitude.

There were no long speeches. The King hates them and has always dreaded having to make one. He was brevity itself. The bridegroom, another sailor, had just as little to say. It was a very large room and there were no microphones, so few people even heard the little that *was* said. The French gentleman kept hissing in my ear, *'Qu'est ce qu'il dit?'* I was unable to help him.

Though they had so much on their minds, and so many to claim their attention that day, both the King and Queen came to look for me. 'Well, Crawfie,' said the King. 'I think she is happy, don't you?' I told him I had no doubt of it. He went on to say how much it had meant to them, my being with them all those years, and he looked, as he spoke, wistfully at the radiant Lilibet.

The Queen kissed me. 'What a wonderful day it has been, Crawfie,' she said.

'Yes, ma'am,' I replied. 'Though I feel as if I, too, had lost a daughter.'

Her Majesty said kindly, 'I am sure you do, Crawfie. They grow up and leave us, and we must make the best of it.'

From the crowds of famous people there that day, one or two stand out in my mind apart from royalty. Lord and Lady Louis Mountbatten made a handsome couple.

Princess, now Queen, Juliana looked handsome too, although she is one of the people the camera is not kind to. In her photographs she never looks as handsome as she is. In real life she has great charm, that comes from a clear skin and a regal carriage, and a charming naturalness sometimes lacking in persons of exalted rank. She does not dress well. On this occasion she wore a magnificent stole with a rose pinned to it. The stole kept slipping so that the rose often blossomed in the most unlikely places. Both she and Prince Bernhard have great courtesy. I have always remembered how, on their way from floor to floor in the Palace lift, they never dreamed of going on and leaving anyone standing. Scottish people all love the Dutch Royal Family. At one time, when Princess Juliana was with her mother in Scotland, they spent their holidays like anyone else, bicycling about the countryside. I always remember Princess Juliana, then quite young, at the Duchess of Kent's wedding, where she was a bridesmaid. She lost a bracelet in the Abbey, which upset her greatly. I helped her look for it, but I don't believe it was ever found.

George and Gerald Lascelles, two rather solemn young men, Lilibet's cousins, came to look for me. 'I expect you are feeling rather sad today, Miss Crawford,' George said sympathetically. At that time he did not know that he himself was to play a leading part in the next royal wedding, when he married pretty little Miss Marion Stein, daughter of an Austrian music publisher.

The younger members of the family and their nannies had a quiet lunch and a nice lie down in another part of the Palace, before reappearing again to see the bride and bridegroom depart. Prince William and Prince Michael, I remember, were thoroughly overtired, grew peevish, and almost came to blows. Shocked nannies enveloped them in those vast white shawls royal nannies always seem to have handy. Like sheltering wings! They were borne off, but not before they had made ceremonious bows to the King and Queen. In royal circles manners are taught young.

Rain had held off during the day, but with evening it became foggy and cold. Lights streaming from the Palace windows were reflected in the wet forecourt where the open landau with its two horses waited to take the young couple away. A closed car would have been a great deal more comfortable and convenient, but all through the gathering twilight the vast crowds had been waiting there patiently, and they must not be disappointed.

Presently Lilibet came running down, in her new powder-blue frock and its matching coat. She wore a beret with a feather cockade the same colour, and looked so happy. Hand in hand she and her new husband ran the gauntlet of paper rose-petals.

We chased their carriage as far as the big gates. The Queen picked up her silk skirts and came right up to the railings with us. For a long time we could hear the cheers rising and falling, as the carriage passed through the crowds that lined the route all the way to Victoria, where fresh crowds packed the station.

It was all over. Suddenly everything was very quiet. In the big banqueting hall footmen were reassembling the gold chairs. Another footman had a small tray laden with lost pieces of jewellery and bracelets which he took down to the Master of the Household to be claimed. The big wedding cakes, twelve of them, were taken away to be sent to hospitals. Only one of them was cut up and posted off to relations and friends. It goes in a larger box than is customary, with the royal coat of arms emblazoned on it.

The King and Queen went to their own apartments, no doubt glad at last to be quiet after all the excitement of the day. They did not go out anywhere that night, but remained together at home. Margaret, still in her bridesmaid's frock, came along presently to my room, where I, too, had been very glad to sit down for a little while and rest. Margaret looked pale and tired, and I thought a little sad.

'Lilibet's gone!' she said. 'Oh, Crawfie, I can't imagine life here without her.'

I couldn't imagine life without her either, and there was a

lump in my throat. 'Never mind,' I said, as brightly as I could. 'You will be the next.'

'Don't be silly, Crawfie,' said Margaret with a brisk return of her old spirit. 'You know quite well Papa and Mummie need me to keep them in order. What would they do without me!'

I kissed her and told her to go and rest. There was a party that night for the bridesmaids and ushers. They dined somewhere, and went on and danced. I sat down to wait for George. I had left him at the Abbey, and I knew he must have been trying to get to the Palace to fetch me. Presently he arrived. We dined quietly in a small café near Victoria Station. Little did the waitress who served us guess where we had spent the rest of that day.

CHAPTER XII

A Nephew for Margaret

THE wedding was over. Margaret now branched out in a life of her own. She was now *the* Princess at the Palace, with more and more parties, and more and more friends, and less and less work! I think at that time both the King and Queen were a little bewildered and worried. They did not know what to do about her. She did not seem to be settling down at all. Of course, the mornings were fully occupied with lessons, but the afternoons were not organized and Princess Margaret had much free time.

About this time I had a serious talk with Queen Mary, who also felt that a campaign should be prepared, to launch Margaret into doing some definite work. All girls were working in those days, and it was to the Palace people looked for example in these things. From time to time it was discussed, but nothing was done. There was now no definite routine, with the result that when Margaret was not with me she mooned about her rooms, getting more and more depressed. She was just one little girl alone in the Palace, with no sister to go about with and nothing much to do, and no one of her own age to play with.

The Press for the moment no longer had Lilibet to gossip about, so they turned their attention to Margaret. The camera followed her round. Her name was linked with half a dozen different young men. If, being young, just at first it amused her and made her feel important, it soon became a nuisance.

'It is the penalty you have to pay for being a princess,' I told her. 'You must just grin and bear it. After all,' I pointed out, 'you can often get a good laugh out of it.' This was indeed the case, especially when a bold bid was made to forge a romance between her and the young King of Rumania, because they once went to the same theatre party, and he lent her his programme. Margaret had found him exceptionally hard to talk to.

Margaret is no more frivolous or flirtatious than any other normal high-spirited and pretty girl of her age, who has been a little spoiled. She is a lot brighter than most. Now and again, through the strain of living in a palace, the constant centre of all eyes, her doings may seem to lack that wisdom and discretion expected of those who live at court. But beneath all her nonsense, Margaret is level-headed far beyond her years. If at times she delights to shock the conventional people around her, she is not the first young person to do that. She is learning with the years to control her sharp tongue, and that bright wit which in the past made worthy old gentlemen write, 'Lilibet is a dear child, but Margaret always makes me uncomfortable.'

She has a definite dress sense. She knows what suits her. When she returned from the African trip she amused everyone by announcing that she would no longer wear her sister's cast-offs, tweed or evening.

It is a grief to her that she is so small, and she wears shoes and hats that give her an extra inch or so. Her vitality is boundless, as those who wait upon her, and her escorts to many a dance, know to their cost.

Margaret's first lady-in-waiting was Jennifer Bevan. She was just Margaret's age, and from the start they had seemed to like each other.

The business of choosing a lady-in-waiting is a very complicated and long-drawn-out affair. It is a lengthy process, and has been known to take as much as two years before a final decision has been come to. By that time, the candidate sometimes is married, or has left the country, and then the fuss starts all over again. The final stage is reached when the prospective lady is invited to tea in the lady-in-waiting's room. It must be quite an ordeal, but anyone who gets as far as that is usually gazetted.

To be lady-in-waiting is a post much sought after, and I don't think anyone has ever refused it when it was offered to them. It is a pleasant job, but often extremely tiring, and royal employers vary immensely in their degrees of considerateness for those who wait upon them. The pay is small – the small salary they receive is really a dress allowance and no more. The duties are those of a personal secretary. Private correspondence is attended to, shopping done, and the lady-in-waiting in attendance must accompany her princess wherever she goes. In Margaret's case this has meant, often enough, dancing all night long.

Late or early the night before, the lady-in-waiting must be in attendance at the Palace next morning as usual. There are letters to be attended to, and a dozen routine jobs that have to be done. Often it is quite a business finding Margaret if she is otherwise engaged.

Margaret is more exacting to work for than Lilibet ever was. Lilibet has always had an orderly mind, and perhaps a firmer grasp of what other people's problems are. She would pencil notes on her letters, saying yes or no. Giving some line on how she wanted them answered. And her lady-in-waiting always knew where, in emergency, she could find her. Margaret was all over the place. She had a wonderful time, but I was very worried about her. I spoke to the Queen quite openly.

'I can do nothing with her. She is tired out, and absolutely exhausted with all these late nights,' I said.

The Queen replied, 'We are only young once, Crawfie. We want her to have a good time. With Lilibet gone, it is lonely for her here.'

This was natural enough, but the newspapers soon got hold of all this, and openly stated that Margaret had been out seven nights in a week. This made a difficult situation. People look to the Royal Family to set them an example, above all in domestic issues, and I feel sure that in many a home this was dragged up to counter parental interference over night life: 'But look what Princess Margaret is allowed to do!'

The King and Queen, I know, both felt that all this gaiety was not entirely desirable, but as always they could not bring themselves to cross her for some time. Then an arrangement was come to, by which she spent one or two nights of every week quietly at home. This was a wise decision, for Margaret was never very strong.

I spoke to her myself more than once on the subject, but it was difficult to get her to take me seriously. I tried, I remember, to make her realize her lady-in-waiting's point of view.

'Other girls have work to do,' I pointed out. 'They can't stay late in bed. They have got to get up in the morning after a dance and catch a bus. They probably have to get their own breakfast.'

And she said, 'Crawfie, even if I wanted to cook my breakfast, I couldn't, because there's nothing here to cook on.' She turns it all into a joke.

Lilibet wrote us all happy little letters, but the first part of the honeymoon, apart from the fact that at last they were together, wasn't any great success. Once more they had no privacy. They were pursued by cameras and ever-watchful eyes. It was up at the quiet little house Birkhall that their real honeymoon began. Birkhall had so many happy memories. The wide moors took them to their hearts. The country folk, with traditional Scottish courtesy, left them alone.

It was nice to know that somebody's married life was beginning full of peace and sunshine. My own was not. George was living meantime in a hotel in South Kensington, for our little house was unlikely to be ready for occupation for some time, and even when the painters were out it needed all kinds of attention in the way of curtains and covers, which I had no time to give.

There seemed little I could do. The King and Queen were often away, and unless I stayed, it meant Margaret was all alone in one wing of the Palace. There was still no talk of my retiring, nor had I any hint of what my future was to be.

There were many new duties, now, for the little Princess who was left. From the time of Lilibet's marriage, a new life began for Margaret also. She entered into it with her usual enthusiasm, and enjoyed every moment of it, but it was a strain on her. She was so very young still, and though not at all shy, she always suffered from nerves when she had to do things by herself.

'I get a sick feeling in my tummy,' she told me. 'Just as I used to before our pantomimes began.'

She overcame it, and never let anyone know, and when in the public eye always appears a very calm and poised young person. Only those of us who know her well realize what she really feels.

I remember her coming to me one day, elated: 'What do you think, Crawfie? I am going to represent Papa and Mummie at Juliana's coronation!' It was her first big undertaking, and probably I was not the only person in the Palace who felt a little apprehensive for her. We had great fun getting her clothes together, and on that occasion I played the governess's part thoroughly and gave her a lot of good advice.

She asked George and me and Jock Colville to meet her at the airport when she came back. The Duke of Beaufort, who, with a lady-in-waiting, had accompanied her, was full of enthusiasm.

'You may well be proud of Her Royal Highness,' he said. 'I have never seen anyone carry off a situation with more dignity and charm. There was not one difficult moment.'

All the way back in the car, we gossiped together. Margaret was enchanted with Holland, and the friendly people who had given her such a wonderful welcome. I told her then that we all felt very proud of her. She gave me that mischievous side glance of hers, half laughter, half solemn.

'Well, I have to behave myself now, Crawfie, don't I? There is no Lilibet around, to keep me in my place with a sisterly poke.'

Around ten o'clock one night, Lilibet appeared at the Palace on her way north from Broadlands, for the second part of her honeymoon. She came rushing along to my room and said, 'Oh, Crawfie, can you find me a dog lead? I have a new puppy!' The King and Queen and Margaret were at Sandringham. 'My horrid sister has taken all the leads out of the Palace,' Lilibet said.

I said I would go to the Queen's rooms and get one of the pages to look in the cupboard, but there wasn't a dog lead of any kind, not even a bit of string. I rushed back to her and said, 'You'll just have to take the belt off my coat and take your dog to the station on the belt, because I can't find a lead or even a bit of string.'

In the end the footman found a very old chewed lead and collar in somebody's drawer, and put it on the new puppy.

Lilibet seemed very happy indeed that night. She was wearing her new beaver coat which had been sent from Canada and was quite lovely and very long. She seemed to me really like somebody's wife. Her whole atmosphere had changed. Even the way she did her hair was different.

Lilibet has real affection for dogs. She loves them and makes friends of them. They have now taken the place of the thirty horses which once stood round the dome. She is very punctilious about having the dogs taken out; they must be taken for a walk in the morning and also in the afternoon. She used to ring me occasionally and say, 'Crawfie, are you doing anything?' And I would say, 'Oh, all right, I'll take the dogs out.' She didn't like to leave them to the footmen in case they took them only to the nearest door and brought them in again.

The Queen also is very fond of dogs, and one of the corgis is devoted to her and won't go to anybody else.

At first it was not certain where Lilibet and Philip would live. One day Lilibet came to me and said, 'Grannie is so sweet. She said to me, "When I die, Lilibet, you will have Marlborough House." But oh dear, we don't at all want Grannie to die. We hope she will be here for a very long time, and we must have a London house before that.'

Later I heard Clarence House had been chosen for them. I don't think they much liked the idea. Clarence House, as it then was, was quite ghastly. Like so much of the royal property, it was gloomy and in bad need of cleaning up and replete with every labour-making device! But it was near Buckingham Palace, and quite centrally located.

Once again the young couple were handicapped by having too much. It is very difficult to fit in wedding presents when there are enough of them to fill a museum, and not everything just what one would personally have chosen. Yet they must be used up.

I think the young couple never took as much interest in Clarence House as they did in planning and arranging their country home, Sunninghill Park, near Ascot. All the

Princesses' happiest times after the 145 Piccadilly days had been spent in the country, either at Royal Lodge, Windsor, or up in Scotland. They hoped to carry on the same tradition and make the same atmosphere in their own home. They had been there together, planning and arranging the house, thrilled with their new home.

In the middle of their honeymoon they got the news that the place had been burned down. This was a grief and disappointment that must have cast a shadow over Lilibet's happiness. I had one hurt letter from her. She had had such love and kindness from people over her marriage, that this turn of affairs left her lost and bewildered.

'Oh, Crawfie, how _could_ it have happened?' she wrote. 'Do you really think someone did it on purpose? I can't believe it. People are always so kind to us. I don't for one moment believe it was the squatters.'

A number of homeless families had been squatting in the disused army camp in the grounds. There was a suggestion that perhaps they had been responsible. It must always be hard for the homeless to see other people making themselves homes. No one ever knew, but I think Lilibet was very deeply hurt over it.

Windlesham Manor, a nice, comfortable, medium-sized house, was next chosen for them by the King. It has lovely gardens, and is conveniently near to both Windsor and London. Here was the young people's real home where they could choose their own way of life and furnish to suit themselves. Official residences are always official residences, and rarely feel like home.

We who loved Lilibet looked forward to the time when she would have an establishment of her own. Buckingham Palace is _not_ the place to be newly married in. Besides, young people, no matter what their circumstances, are better off, once married, away from their parents. For a while Lilibet continued her childhood's habit, and always went down to the Queen to ask, 'Shall I do this?' or 'Do you approve of that?'

Gradually she became more self-reliant, and in this her husband has been a great help to her. I think he has brought her more into touch with the outside world, and a more natural and unconventional life than court life can ever be. People at Broadlands, where they spent the first part of their honeymoon, still talk of a bright blue jeep that tore through the town one day (no doubt a lot too fast). In it sat a girl, bare-headed with blowing hair, and a young man in an open-necked shirt. Both singing!

When Lilibet and her husband came back from their honeymoon they had a suite in the Palace temporarily until their own house was ready for them. Philip had a job at the Admiralty and went off to work every morning just like any other young husband, often walking down the Mall to the office. Both Lilibet and Margaret found this enchanting. Around four-thirty in the afternoon, Lilibet would stand look-ing out of the window, waiting, if not exactly to hear the gate click, to see the tall, lean figure coming past the fountain in the centre of the road outside the Palace, or to see his small sports car turn in at the Palace gates. Usually a deal too fast.

It was rather charming to see the way Margaret adapted herself to this new state of affairs, and treated the sister she had teased and mimicked with new deference. As though for the first time she realized that here was not only the ever-kindly Lilibet who had, like everyone else, been inclined to spoil her and give in to her, but the future Queen of England.

My little cottage had now been done up and was quite delight-ful, but it still had a very odd, antiquated boiler. From time to time the temperature would rise suddenly and inexplicably, and the water boil so furiously that I lived in constant terror it would burst. I would hastily run the hot water off, and then, unwilling to waste so much, I used to have a bath. Sometimes at unusual hours, all depending on the mood of this boiler.

One evening, just as I had finished this performance, the door-bell rang. In a dressing-gown and bath cap, I went to see who my caller was, and found Philip and Lilibet on the door-step. They looked at me in utter astonishment, and Lilibet said:

'What on earth are you doing, Crawfie! We came to pay you our official call.'

I explained the situation. Philip went to have a look at my temperamental hot-water system, with a sailor's interest in curious mechanical gadgets. They went all over my little house with me, looked in cupboards, and took a very great interest in it all. Then they both sat on my kitchen table and talked to me while I prepared my solitary supper. My husband was at that time in hospital.

Margaret had measles. She had a severe attack and had to stay in bed for some time. She had a night nurse and a day nurse who were sisters at the Great Ormond Street Hospital for Sick Children. They came to look after her in fear and trembling, remembering current rumours and gossip, and thinking they would have a naughty little patient to nurse. They found instead this delightful child who, like any other child who is sick, depended solely on the kindness of the people around.

They greatly enjoyed their month or six weeks with her. When she was better she used to go in when they were having their supper, or they would come in to her, and she would teach them to dance the Scottish reels.

After I was settled, she rang up one day to say, 'Crawfie, I would like you to have the two sisters to Nottingham Cottage for tea, and I shall come and have tea with them.'

I arranged it, and the sisters came. Princess Margaret

arrived soon after, and we had the merriest of tea parties. She went over all the jokes they had had together, and was completely charming.

Hardly had the young couple returned to London than the journalistic speculations began. Was Lilibet or was she not going to have a baby? I knew it was her dearest wish, and that she hoped to be a mother before her first wedding anniversary, but it was not a subject she cared to have the whole world speculating on. These are personal and sacred matters which everyone save royalty can keep to themselves.

'Probably we shall read about it in the papers before we really know ourselves,' Lilibet said dryly, but rather sadly.

Then one day Lilibet came to my room and told me, 'I think I am going to have a baby, Crawfie.' She was frightfully pleased. That was the thing she wanted most.

I said, 'Do you remember when you were small you said you would have lots of babies, two girls and two boys?'

The newspapers got hold of the news almost at once. They even published the date of the birth, usually quite wrong. No one knows just how it is these things leak out. There must be some form of jungle or bush telegraph that operates in the Palace and has not yet been discovered. Once again Lilibet's correspondence grew in volume, letters from kindly people giving her good advice on how to manage her pregnancy, and many an old wife divulged to her the magic spells by which she might know whether she would have a son or a daughter.

Margaret in those months was touchingly solicitous for her sister. Long before the time came for Lilibet to have her feet up or need cushions at her back, Margaret was around after her, taking care of her.

'Lilibet, you really mustn't run with the dogs like that. Not now,' she would reprove her.

Lilibet remained remarkably strong and active the whole

time. She has really wonderful health. Not very long before her baby came, Lady Hyde told me, laughing, how one morning she was on her way to see the Queen and saw Lilibet in the corridor ahead of her. Lilibet looked round, and obviously thinking, 'I must get in first,' she picked up her skirts and did a brisk sprint out of sight.

The coming of a baby brings the feel of spring into the most gloomy household. Once again, everything was made new. The old pram in which Alah had firmly penned Margaret for so long came back from its purdah. It was sent away to be done up. When it came back, Lilibet brought it down to my room one day when no one was about. The door opened and slowly she manoeuvred it in.

'Look, Crawfie, I'm getting my hand in.'

Later I saw Bobo, who had been Lilibet's nursemaid, having a turn with it, no doubt reviving memories of old days. The cot and the baby's basket appeared. These are more or less heirlooms and are refurbished again and again.

The Royal Family do not observe the old tradition of pink and blue. The cot and basket were done up in buttercup-yellow silk, with lace trimmings.

'Then no one can guess whether we want a boy or a girl,' Lilibet explained. 'Fancy a poor little girl turning up and finding a blue-for-a-boy cot waiting for her!'

Once again, presents began to arrive; and once again the old convention was given the go-by and Lilibet kept whatever was sent her. Baby clothes from all over the world came from all manner of people. Shawls were knitted by the dozen. Piles of matinee coats and bootees mounted up. What Lilibet could not use were made up into layettes for other young mothers whose babies came at the same time.

A touching thing was the number of letters that came from German mothers who wrote, 'From the depths of our hearts we share your happiness in this,' and went on to tell how much they always admired the King and Queen of England and their children, and liked to have news of them.

These letters were all sent to the Foreign Office and I think all of them were answered. Perhaps it is a good omen for England that the little Prince made those bonds of good feeling between one-time enemies, even before he was born.

Parcels of beautiful baby clothes came from America, and with them were always charming cards of greetings to new babies and their mothers, and pictures of storks. Queen Mary sent round a little note once again, begging Lilibet not to throw any of these cards away but to let her have them for her scrapbooks. Every Christmas Her Majesty diligently rounds up all the family Christmas cards, and these are made up into books that delight the children in many a hospital ward.

Besides letters of congratulations and friendliness, there were hundreds filled with other people's problems, sent to her in the mistaken notion that a princess can do anything she likes, and has but to express a wish to have it granted. A woman wrote, 'My son is in prison. He has been there three years. You who are now so happy in expecting a baby could have him released for me.' These were all sorted out as best might be. Letters of this sort can never be answered by any member of the Royal Family personally, but have to be dealt with officially. They all went to the Home Office.

After the baby came, a special department had to be opened in the Palace, and a dozen typists engaged temporarily to cope with the flood of mail we could no longer handle. It was not only letters and telegrams. People sent their baby's birth certificate, registered, to prove their child had been born at the same moment as the little Prince. Some of these came from Germany and from France, as well as America, and all had to be duly returned.

I continued to leave my little cottage in Kensington every morning, and go to the Palace, where I often remained until late at night. There was so much to do, and my own home life had to remain meantime in abeyance. In what spare time I had, I struggled with the problem of my own curtains and covers, and the hundred-and-one things that have to be done when one settles into a new home.

Queen Mary was most helpful to me. One day when I was speaking to her of some of my difficulties, she got up and crossed to her bureau, and wrote down for me the name of a man in Fulham Road who did small repairs very cheaply.

'There you are, my dear,' said Her Majesty. 'You will find him *most* useful.'

I found the card the other day among my papers, and it brought those days back to me again. It was Queen Mary who gave me the beautiful flower prints that hang in my little house, as well as many most useful pieces of Victorian furniture. When Queen Mary gives a present she does the thing thoroughly. First, the pictures were delivered. Next, a man came round to hang them. Then came Queen Mary herself, to see that the job had been properly done.

Margaret still did an occasional hour's work with me, but she was now going about more and more, continuing to attract the notice and comment that had once been reserved for her sister. Unfortunately, in Margaret's case it was often unkind. Impulsive and bright remarks she made became headlines and, taken out of their context, began to produce in the public eye an oddly distorted personality that bore little resemblance to the Margaret we knew.

Lilibet spent many happy hours getting her baby's nursery ready at Clarence House. It had cream walls and a blue carpet, and enchanting cream-coloured chintz with red nursery-rhyme figures all over it. It had its own miniature bathroom, with bath, towel-rails, and bath towels all to scale. Lilibet's old nursery-china cupboard was moved over there. It was packed with the small ornaments she had always loved so dearly herself – little soldiers, little mice, little coaches, and whole families of teddy bears they had got at Lady Astor's children's parties long ago, and had carefully kept ever since. Everything was very hygienic. All the cupboards lighted up inside when the doors were opened.

During those months before her baby was born, Lilibet often came to talk to me, sometimes in my room at the Palace, sometimes at my own home. She was a serene and very happy little mother. She never lost her looks.

There had been a good deal of discussion as to where the child would be born. Both the King and Queen were anxious to have her move over to the other and quieter side of the Palace, overlooking the gardens and the lake. We knew that crowds, which are a part of any happening in the Royal Family, would gather under the windows and fill the Mall as usual, with the attendant clamour and noise that goes on all night.

Lilibet, however, was quite firm, and for once stood out against the family and put her foot down. 'I want my baby to be born in my own room, amongst the things I know,' she said.

It was November, getting foggy and dark. The last days dragged, as they always do. Lilibet rang me up at my cottage one afternoon and said she was coming to tea with me.

The car drove up at five o'clock, and Lilibet came in. She looked so well, and so very happy. She wore a pretty navy-blue maternity dress, with a white trimming that looked, at first, like lace, until you saw it was all done in little white beads.

There was a very special sort of chocolate cake that I knew was a favourite of hers. It can be bought in only one place in London, and with great good fortune I had managed to get one. Lilibet ate a large tea worthy of our old schoolroom days. We laughed a lot, and spoke of old friends, and remembered our first meeting, and those early days together.

I kept looking at her, and saying, 'I can hardly believe that you are really going to have a baby. It seems incredible to me. Are you frightened at all, Lilibet? What do you feel about it?'

She told me she had complete faith in her doctor, and was, if anything, looking forward to the experience. 'After all, it is what we're made for,' she said philosophically.

I was much struck by her conversation. She seemed so interested in everything that was going on, and so very well informed. My husband joined us before we finished tea, and he was deeply impressed by all she knew of India and Ceylon, where he had spent many years.

At last she got up, and kissed me. 'Well, Crawfie dear, I suppose I must go home,' she said. She looked rather thoughtfully round my little sitting room. I knew she was thinking that perhaps next time she saw it, her ordeal would be over and she would be a mother.

It became evident that the baby's arrival would take place over the weekend of 13 November. Margaret had arranged to go away the week before. When she heard this news she wanted to stay at home. She was extremely anxious about her sister.

'Don't worry yourself,' I told her. 'A baby is born every minute, and many of the mothers are not by any means as healthy as your sister.'

In the end it was decided she should stick to her original plan, and she departed. But I was told when I returned to the Palace on Monday that she had rung up every half-hour or so over the weekend.

On Sunday, 14 November I had a telephone message from the Palace informing me that Her Royal Highness had had a son.

Her nurse took me to see the baby when it was four days old. I had seen most of the royal babies shortly after they were born. They all have a strong resemblance to King George V. Like the little Kents and the little Gloucesters, this baby also had that absurdly mature look, and ridges under his eyes. He was very healthy and strong, and beautifully made, with a flawless, silky skin. The stories that went around at that time about him were entirely without foundation of any kind, born of the strange campaign of secrecy that had grown up of later years. For a long time no pictures were issued, and even the household did not know what the baby's names were to be.

Margaret, besides the excitement of suddenly being an aunt, had been busily preparing for a tour of Australia with the King and Queen. This she had passionately looked forward to, and she had taken a great deal of trouble over her outfit, as usual. The African tour had given her a great taste for travel.

Those of us who were constantly in the Palace had thought the King looked tired and ill, but had put it down to the excitement of the wedding, and the birth of his first grandchild. So that the news of how bad he really was came as an immense shock to all of us. He must have known for some time how ill he was, and as usual he had refused to face it, had carried on till the baby was safely born, and then, probably, had hoped he would somehow manage to get through the Australian tour. But the time came when he had to listen to his doctors, and give in.

Margaret told me, 'When Papa decided he could no longer struggle to keep going, he went to sleep for two days.'

The Australian tour was abandoned. There was bitter disappointment in the colonies, and those other places that would have been visited – but nowhere was it any more bitter than that felt by Margaret. There were anxious days when it was known there would be an operation. They had had, on the whole, so little illness in the family, and always tended to overlook it when they could. But now it had to be faced. The

Queen was quite distraught with anxiety. She could speak, and think, of nothing else, until the operation was safely over.

Life settled down again. But now the pattern was changed. Lilibet had become Mummie, her tall husband was Papa. While Margaret was lovingly labelled by the public 'Charley's Aunt'.

'Probably my proudest title of all,' she said.

It is amusing, now, to look back over the years with all their problems, and festivities, and splendours, and trials. I have so many memories, grave and gay. But to me the best one of all is of a Scottish garden, with the moors behind, wine red, and the air full of the scent of wood smoke, and gorse warmed by the sun, on a summer's morning.

And coming over the garden towards me, three figures, all dressed in blue. The little Duchess and her two daughters, as I knew them first, long ago.